AI Ethics

Status of the Present, Ethical Dilemmas, and Frameworks for the Practical Mind

By

Debbie Sue Jancis

Dedication

To all the incredible teams I have had the privilege of leading and managing throughout my career in the tech sector—your dedication, collaboration, and talent have inspired me every step of the way.

A heartfelt thank you to my loving husband, Paul, and my wonderful children, David, Adam, and Rebecca, and my brother, Michael. Your unwavering support and encouragement have made this journey possible. Thank you for constantly pushing me to keep writing and sharing my passion.

Lastly, this book is dedicated to the future of AI. May we strive to design and implement ethical, transparent, fair, and equitable AI systems for all, ensuring that technology serves humanity with integrity and respect.

Table of Contents

Introduction

Imagine waking to a gentle nudge from your smart bed, having monitored your sleep cycles to find the perfect moment for you to rise, refreshed. Your smart home greets you with a soft, warm light as the aroma of freshly brewed coffee, tailored to your precise taste and health needs, fills the air. As you sip, your personal AI assistant outlines your day, organizing it for maximum efficiency and balance, factoring in your work commitments, fitness routine, and even carving out time for relaxation and hobbies.

Outside, autonomous vehicles whisk people to their destinations, navigating a harmonious flow of traffic that's been meticulously optimized to reduce accidents and congestion. Drones buzz overhead, delivering packages with pinpoint accuracy, while robots in the distance tend to fields, harvesting crops engineered for sustainability and nutrition. In hospitals, AI-driven diagnostics and treatments offer hope with precision medicine, crafting therapies uniquely suited to each patient's genetic makeup.

Yet, beneath this utopia, the seeds of a chilling dystopia take root. In the shadows, the same intelligence that orchestrates your perfect day holds the potential to surveil and control, its algorithms opaque and its decisions unchallengeable. Initially designed as humanity's servant, this omnipresent AI could become its overseer, with the power to manipulate economies, influence elections, and dictate personal freedoms. Here, in the delicate balance between utopian dreams and dystopian warnings, lies our collective future with AI, a future that hinges on the ethical choices we make today.

Every time you watch a blockbuster movie showcasing AI as menacing robots with world domination plans, remember that such portrayals are more about entertainment than artificial intelligence's accurate capabilities or moral challenges. AI's current achievements are profoundly transformative yet grounded in a complex ethical landscape that seldom makes it to the silver screen. My vision for our future—one where robust ethical principles guide AI's development—aims to avert the dystopian scenarios popular culture often presents and instead harness AI's potential to enhance our world significantly.

This book invites you on a comprehensive journey that begins with AI's historical roots, moves through its current accomplishments, and explores the ethical intricacies of its future advancements. We will explore layers of technical insights and ethical evaluations and provide pragmatic guidance tailored for you, the professionals shaping the next era of AI.

The necessity for ethical frameworks in AI development has never been more pronounced. Recent incidents where AI applications faltered due to ethical oversights underline this urgency. Conversely, there are inspiring instances where ethically conscious AI initiatives have propelled positive societal impacts. These stories are lessons and a call to elevate our approach to AI development.

A defining encounter sparked my passion for AI and its ethical dimensions during my early professional years, where I witnessed firsthand the potential repercussions of oversight in AI applications. This experience cemented my dedication to ensuring that future AI professionals could have a guide, a beacon to help navigate these waters.

This book is not just timely but essential. As AI advances, the ethical dilemmas it introduces become more complex and intertwined with every aspect of our lives. This bridges the realms of AI fiction and reality, advocating for an informed and ethically aware approach to AI development.

It targets you, the programmers, project managers, and ethicists entrenched in AI development, and the end users using products and services that AI built into them. It aims to equip you with a nuanced understanding of AI ethics. Here, you will find practical frameworks for ethical decision-making and a vision for fostering sustainable, responsible AI development and how it is used.

As we step forward, I invite you to join this exploration with an open mind and a commitment to ethical innovation. Together, let's prepare to confront and navigate the complexities of AI ethics, ensuring our future is driven by technology and defined by our shared human values. Let this be your call to action, to not just participate in but actively shape the ethical frontier of AI where AI enhances human capabilities and addresses pressing global challenges, all while upholding the highest ethical standards.

Chapter 1: Understanding AI Ethics

In the bustling early days of computer science, few imagined that the machines they programmed to solve equations might one day be subjects of ethical scrutiny. Yet, as these systems have grown in complexity and capability, artificial intelligence has not only transformed technological landscapes but also posed unique moral challenges, necessitating a deep dive into what we now refer to as AI ethics. This chapter aims to unfold the intricate tapestry of AI ethics, tracing its roots from mere concepts to a pivotal element in contemporary AI development. Through this exploration, you will understand how ethical considerations have become integral to technological innovation and the diverse global perspectives that shape these principles.

1.1 The History and Evolution of AI Ethics

Historical Milestones

Artificial Intelligence (AI) is a branch of computer science dedicated to creating systems that can perform tasks that typically require human intelligence. These tasks include reasoning, learning, problem-solving, perception, language understanding, and creativity.

AI systems are designed to simulate human intelligence processes. This simulation involves several components:

- **Learning:** The process of acquiring information and understanding how to apply it.

- **Reasoning:** The process of applying rules to draw approximate or precise conclusions.

- **Self-correction**: Enhancements based on past errors and successes.

Early AI Concepts

The concept of artificial intelligence (AI) traces back to the myths and automatons of ancient civilizations. In Greek mythology, one of the earliest concepts of a synthetic being is Talos, a giant bronze man created by the god Hephaestus. Talos was designed to protect the island of Crete by circling the island's shores three times daily and throwing stones at approaching enemy ships.

Around 1495, Leonardo da Vinci designed a mechanical knight, also known as Leonardo's Robot. This automaton was created as an armored humanoid figure that could perform several human-like motions such as standing, sitting, and moving its arms, possibly even having the ability to open and close its mouth. This invention showcased the early fascination and exploration of human-like machines, indicating the initial steps toward robotics and automation.

These early concepts and myths set a foundation for the modern fascination with creating intelligent machines, bridging mythology, and early engineering explorations with contemporary AI and robotics. They highlight humanity's longstanding intrigue with replicating life and intelligence through artificial means.

Key prominent historical philosophers like René Descartes and Gottfried Wilhelm Leibniz pondered the nature of intelligence, consciousness, and the possibility of artificial beings. This work laid the early theoretical foundations that influenced later developments in computer science and AI, raising fundamental questions about the nature of thought, consciousness, and the potential for artificial minds.

Descartes is known for the dualism theory and his famous quote, "Je pense, donc je suis," or "I think, therefore I am," highlighting the role of thought and consciousness. He influenced the development of AI by laying the groundwork for understanding intelligence as a separate entity from physical form. He also thought that complex systems, like robots, could be created to mimic human actions.

Leibniz developed binary code, the primary language of Computers, and created the basic idea of algorithms. His vision of universal language and a calculating machine was the precursor to a programmable computer. His work laid the early theoretical foundations that influenced later developments in computer science and AI, raising fundamental questions about the nature of thought, consciousness, and the potential for artificial minds.

Birth and early years (1950's – 1960's)

AI's scientific foundation was laid in the mid-20th century. The seminal event was the 1956 Dartmouth Conference, where emeritus Stanford professor John McCarthy coined the term "artificial intelligence," setting the stage for AI as a formal discipline. Many consider this the official birth of AI. At this gathering, McCarthy, Nathaniel Rochester, and Claude Shannon proposed that "every aspect of learning or any other feature of intelligence can in principle be so precisely described that a machine can be made to simulate it" (McCarthy et al., 1956). This bold assertion ignited a wave of optimism, leading to significant early experiments like the creation of ELIZA. This was the first program that allowed some plausible conversation between humans and machines, named for the fictional Eliza Doolittle from George Barnard Shaw's 1913 play Pygmalion and chess-playing programs, which demonstrated rudimentary understanding and problem-solving skills.

Modern AI

The genesis of modern AI can be traced back to the mid-20th century, marked by Alan Turing's groundbreaking work, which posed the question, "Can machines think?" This sparked a series of technological advancements and philosophical debates that laid the groundwork for AI ethics. The real turning point came with the development of more complex algorithms and the deployment of AI in various sectors such as law enforcement, healthcare, and finance, where decisions made by AI systems began affecting human lives directly.

It was incidents like the 1979 NORAD computer malfunction, where an AI mistakenly indicated a potential attack of 1,400 Soviet ICBMs. This error occurred when a lieutenant colonel accidentally loaded a war games tape into a missile warning component of the Worldwide Military Command and Control System (WIMEX). The crisis was averted when additional system checks revealed the truth: it was a false alarm.

A similar incident occurred in 1983. The Soviet nuclear early warning system (Oko) detected the launch of one intercontinental ballistic missile from the United States, followed by four more. Suspecting a false alarm, the engineer on duty waited for corroborating evidence, which never came. Subsequent investigation confirmed that the satellite warning system had malfunctioned. These incidents highlighted the dire need for ethical frameworks in AI systems to avoid catastrophic outcomes.

Ethical Evolution

The introduction of machine learning and deep learning marked a significant shift in AI research. The availability of powerful computing resources and big data has driven the rapid advancement of these technologies.

During this time, there was widespread application and integration. AI has become integral to various industries, including healthcare, automotive, finance, and more, vastly improving efficiencies and capabilities.

There were also some significant milestones during this time period:

- **IBM's Deep Blue defeats Garry Kasparov in chess (1997).**
- **IBM's Watson (2011)** made TV history by defeating the TV quiz show's two foremost all-time champions, Brad Rutter and Ken Jennings.
- **Google's AlphaGo defeats Lee Sedol in Go (2016)**: This was a landmark event, demonstrating the superior problem-solving capabilities of AI in an exceedingly complex game.

The initial discussions about AI ethics were largely theoretical, confined to academic circles and speculative fiction. However, as AI systems became more prevalent in everyday applications—from predictive policing to credit scoring—the discourse shifted from theoretical to urgent. Ethical considerations in AI have evolved to address the unintended consequences of AI decisions and the intentional misuse of AI technologies. Establishing various ethics boards within major tech companies and adopting AI ethics guidelines by governments and international bodies illustrate this shift. This transformation underscores a growing acknowledgment that ethical frameworks must be integral to AI development rather than an afterthought.

Influential Figures

Several thinkers have significantly shaped the discourse on AI ethics. Alan Turing, often hailed as the father of theoretical computer science and artificial intelligence, first introduced the ethical dimensions of machine intelligence.

Allen Newell and Herbert A. Simon were pivotal figures in the development of artificial intelligence and cognitive psychology. Their collaborative work at the RAND Corporation and later at Carnegie Mellon University led to groundbreaking advancements in understanding human thought processes and the creation of AI. Newell and Simon developed the Logic Theorist, which is considered the first artificial intelligence program capable of proving mathematical theorems.

Their most significant contribution was the development of the General Problem Solver (GPS), a universal problem-solving machine that laid the foundation for future AI research. Simon's work in bounded rationality and decision-making earned him the Nobel Prize in Economics in 1978, highlighting his interdisciplinary influence. Both Newell and Simon emphasized the importance of understanding human cognition to create more effective and human-like artificial intelligence, significantly shaping the fields of cognitive psychology, AI, and computer science.

Joseph Weizenbaum and Norbert Wiener were pioneering figures in the fields of computer science and cybernetics, respectively. Weizenbaum, a German-American computer scientist, is best known for creating ELIZA, one of the earliest natural language processing programs. This program simulated a Rogerian (person-centered theory) psychotherapist by rephrasing certain parts of the user's input as questions. His work highlighted the ethical implications of artificial intelligence, leading him to advocate for responsible AI development and caution against over-reliance on computers.

Norbert Wiener, an American mathematician and philosopher, is often regarded as the father of cybernetics—the interdisciplinary study of control and communication in animals, humans, and machines. His groundbreaking book, "Cybernetics: Or Control and Communication in the Animal and the Machine," laid the theoretical foundations for modern systems theory and automation, profoundly influencing fields ranging from engineering to the social sciences.

Both Weizenbaum and Wiener were deeply concerned with the societal and ethical impacts of technological advancements, emphasizing the need for human oversight and ethical considerations in developing and deploying intelligent systems.

In recent years, figures such as Joy Buolamwini, who founded the Algorithmic Justice League, have brought attention to issues of bias and fairness in AI through her work on the Gender Shades project, which evaluates the performance of AI facial recognition technologies across different genders and skin tones. These individuals have advanced the technical dimensions of AI and steered the conversation towards its ethical implications.

Global Perspectives

The ethical considerations of AI are not confined to any single cultural or national boundary; they are as diverse as the global community itself. For instance, European approaches to AI ethics tend to emphasize privacy and data protection, heavily influenced by the General Data Protection Regulation (GDPR). In contrast, in the United States, there is a stronger focus on mitigating bias and ensuring fairness, reflecting the country's ongoing struggles with racial and social inequalities. Meanwhile, in Asian countries like Japan and China, the integration of AI ethics also considers societal harmony and collective well-being, influenced by broader socio-cultural norms. This variety of perspectives ensures a richer, more comprehensive understanding of what ethical AI can mean across different global contexts.

Understanding these diverse approaches is essential for creating AI systems that are technically proficient, culturally sensitive, and ethically sound. As AI continues to evolve and integrate into every facet of our global society, the insights from these diverse perspectives will be invaluable in guiding the ethical development of AI technologies.

1.2 Fundamental Ethical Theories Applied to AI

As we pivot from the historical and global contexts of AI ethics to the foundational theories that support ethical decision-making in AI, it becomes crucial to dissect how traditional ethical theories apply to the nuanced realm of artificial intelligence. The development and deployment of AI technologies challenge us to rethink these age-old theories in the light of new digital realities. In this exploration, we delve into four cardinal ethical theories—Utilitarianism, Deontological Ethics, Virtue Ethics, and Pragmatic Ethics—and interpret how each can be intricately woven into the fabric of AI development to guide ethical AI creation.

Utilitarianism in AI

Utilitarianism, a theory in normative ethics developed by philosophers like Jeremy Bentham and John Stuart Mill, advocates that actions are justified if they maximize happiness and minimize suffering for the most significant number of people. When applied to AI, this principle pushes for the creation of technologies that chiefly aim to increase efficiency and enhance well-being on a large scale.

For instance, AI-driven healthcare platforms designed to optimize patient treatment plans embody this principle by aiming to improve health outcomes for the largest number of patients. Similarly, in public policy, AI can assist in creating models that predict the societal impact of various decisions, helping policymakers choose options that enhance overall welfare.

The utilitarian approach encourages developers to consider the broader implications of AI technologies, promoting solutions that deliver the most significant positive impact.

However, utilitarianism in AI also raises critical questions: What defines happiness in the context of AI? How do we measure it, and whose happiness is prioritized? The primary issue is quantifying and comparing happiness or satisfaction across different individuals and groups, which can be inherently subjective. AI systems may struggle to balance competing interests and values, leading to ethical dilemmas.

For example, imagine an AI-powered job recruitment system faced with selecting candidates for limited job openings. The system might need to decide between prioritizing candidates with the highest qualifications or those from underrepresented groups, raising questions about fairness and societal benefit. These scenarios highlight the complexity of implementing utilitarian principles in AI, necessitating careful consideration and robust ethical guidelines.

Moreover, utilitarianism in AI must address the risk of unintended consequences and biases. AI systems trained on historical data might perpetuate existing inequalities, inadvertently causing harm rather than maximizing happiness. To mitigate these risks, ensure transparency, fairness, and accountability in AI development. Incorporating diverse perspectives and continuously evaluating AI systems' impact can help align them more closely with utilitarian ideals, fostering technologies that genuinely enhance human well-being.

These are vital considerations, as AI developers might inadvertently prioritize efficiency or the happiness of the majority while overshadowing minority rights or individual suffering. Thus, while utilitarianism can guide AI toward beneficial outcomes for the majority, it necessitates a careful balance to avoid sacrificing the needs of the few.

Utilitarianism offers a valuable ethical framework for guiding AI development and deployment, emphasizing actions that maximize overall happiness. While it provides a clear goal for AI systems, practical implementation requires careful consideration of complex ethical dilemmas, potential biases, and unintended consequences. By addressing these challenges, developers and policymakers can harness AI's potential to improve human welfare in a manner consistent with utilitarian principles.

Deontological Ethics

In contrast to utilitarianism's focus on outcomes, Deontological Ethics, rooted in the work of Immanuel Kant, is a normative ethical theory that emphasizes the importance of duty and adherence to moral rules or principles. Unlike consequentialism, which focuses on the outcomes of actions, deontological ethics asserts that the morality of an action is intrinsically linked to whether it follows a set of predefined rules or duties, regardless of the consequences.

In the realm of AI, this translates into rigid adherence to ethical codes and regulations designed to protect individual rights and ensure that AI systems operate under clearly defined moral duties. For instance, an AI system handling personal data must adhere strictly to rules ensuring user consent and data privacy, reflecting a deontological commitment to user rights and the intrinsic wrongness of privacy violations.

Deontological ethics serves as a crucial counterbalance to AI's outcome-focused approaches, embedding a layer of moral safety that protects individual rights even when pursuing broader beneficial outcomes.

Deontological ethics can provide a robust framework for guiding the development and deployment of AI systems. By emphasizing the importance of ethical principles, developers and policymakers can ensure that AI technologies adhere to fundamental moral values such as fairness, honesty, and respect for human rights. For example, a deontological approach to AI might involve creating algorithms that uphold privacy and data protection principles, ensuring that AI systems do not engage in actions that violate individual privacy rights, regardless of the potential benefits.

One of the key strengths of deontological ethics in AI is its emphasis on consistency and predictability. Following moral rules allows AI systems to offer more transparent and understandable decision-making processes. This predictability is crucial in applications such as autonomous vehicles, healthcare, and legal systems, where adherence to ethical standards is paramount. For instance, in healthcare, deontological principles might dictate that AI systems must always seek informed consent from patients before using their data, thereby respecting their autonomy and dignity.

However, deontological ethics also presents challenges when applied to AI. One significant issue is the potential for conflict between different moral duties or principles. For example, an AI system designed to uphold the duty of honesty might face a situation where telling the truth could cause harm, leading to a conflict between the principles of honesty and non-maleficence (the duty to "do no harm"). Additionally, rigid adherence to rules can sometimes lead to morally questionable outcomes if the rules are flawed or fail to account for complex, nuanced situations.

Moreover, the static nature of deontological rules can be problematic in the rapidly evolving field of AI, where new ethical dilemmas and unforeseen consequences frequently arise. To address these challenges, it is essential to incorporate mechanisms for continuous ethical evaluation and adaptation within AI systems. By combining deontological principles with other ethical approaches, such as virtue ethics or consequentialism, developers can create more comprehensive and flexible ethical frameworks that better navigate the complexities of AI.

Deontological ethics offers a valuable perspective for guiding AI systems' ethical development and deployment, emphasizing adherence to moral rules and principles. While it provides a clear and consistent ethical framework, practical implementation requires careful consideration of potential conflicts between duties and the need for adaptability in the face of new ethical challenges. By integrating deontological ethics with other ethical approaches, AI can be developed to uphold fundamental moral values while addressing the dynamic and complex nature of technological innovation.

Virtue Ethics

Virtue ethics, rooted in Aristotle's philosophical traditions, shifts the focus from the action to the moral agent's character and virtues, in this case, both the AI system and its creators. It emphasizes these virtues over strict rules or consequences. Unlike deontological ethics, which focuses on duties, and utilitarianism, which focuses on outcomes, virtue ethics centers on developing good character traits or virtues, such as courage, wisdom, temperance, and justice. The primary aim is cultivating a moral character that enables individuals to make wise and ethical decisions naturally, promoting human flourishing and well-being.

This theory encourages the cultivation of virtues such as honesty, kindness, and loyalty. Translated into AI development, this means creating systems that perform tasks and do so in a way that aligns with virtuous behavior. For example, an AI designed for educational purposes should effectively teach and support virtues like fairness and patience, encouraging similar traits in its users. The challenge here lies in programming AI systems that understand these virtues and embody them in their operations, pushing developers to consider what their AI does and how it does it in various scenarios.

In artificial intelligence (AI), virtue ethics offers a unique and human-centric approach to ethical considerations. This perspective encourages AI developers and designers to focus on fostering virtues within AI systems and in the interactions between humans. For example, an AI designed with virtue ethics in mind might prioritize fostering empathy, fairness, and transparency, ensuring that its actions and decisions promote the well-being of individuals and society. This approach can guide the creation of AI systems that support ethical behavior, encourage positive human interactions, and enhance the moral development of users.

One of the key advantages of virtue ethics in AI is its flexibility and adaptability. Instead of rigidly following predefined rules or focusing solely on outcomes, virtue ethics allows for a more nuanced and context-sensitive approach to ethical decision-making. This is particularly valuable in complex and dynamic environments where AI systems operate, such as healthcare, education, and social services. By promoting virtues like compassion and prudence, AI systems can better navigate ethical dilemmas and provide solutions that align with the holistic well-being of individuals and communities.

However, applying virtue ethics to AI also presents challenges. One significant issue is defining and operationalizing virtues in a way that AI systems can understand and embody. Unlike humans, AI lacks intrinsic moral character and cannot develop virtues through lived experience. Therefore, it is crucial to design algorithms and decision-making frameworks that can approximate virtuous behavior, often by incorporating human oversight and continuous ethical evaluation. Additionally, balancing different virtues in practice is challenging, as some situations may require prioritizing one virtue over another, leading to potential conflicts.

Moreover, virtue ethics emphasizes the role of moral exemplars and communities in fostering virtuous behavior. In the context of AI, this suggests the importance of involving diverse and ethically-minded stakeholders in the design and deployment processes. AI developers can ensure that the systems they create reflect a wide range of virtues and ethical considerations by engaging ethicists, sociologists, and the broader public. This collaborative approach can help build AI technologies that are not only technically advanced but also aligned with society's moral values and aspirations.

Virtue ethics provides a valuable framework for guiding the ethical development and use of AI, focusing on cultivating moral virtues and promoting human flourishing. While it presents unique challenges, such as defining virtues for AI and balancing them in practice, its flexibility and emphasis on character offer a rich and human-centered perspective.

By integrating virtue ethics into AI development, we can create technologies that perform tasks efficiently and contribute positively to our communities' moral and social fabric.

Pragmatic Ethics

Lastly, Pragmatic Ethics, which emphasizes practical outcomes and flexible moral principles, is particularly adaptable to the ever-evolving field of AI. This ethical approach advocates for continuous ethical reassessment of AI technologies, adapting to new information and contexts to achieve the most practical and morally sound outcomes. It supports an iterative development process where AI systems are constantly updated and re-evaluated to better align with ethical standards as they change over time. For instance, an AI system used for loan approvals should be regularly updated to reflect current ethical standards on fairness and anti-discrimination, ensuring that its decision-making processes remain just and equitable in the face of societal changes.

In weaving these ethical theories into the fabric of AI development, we are challenged to continuously engage with these concepts, applying them not as static rules but as dynamic guides that evolve alongside AI technology. This ongoing engagement with ethical theories ensures that AI development is about advancing technology and elevating the moral standards by which this technology operates, shaping a future where AI serves humanity justly and wisely.

1.3 AI Ethics: Beyond the Theoretical

Applying theoretical ethical concepts to the tangible realm of AI development often unveils a landscape riddled with complexities that challenge even the most seasoned developers. It's one thing to discuss ethical frameworks in a classroom or conference setting; it's entirely another to integrate these principles into the actual design, development, and deployment of AI systems. Each phase of AI development presents unique challenges and requires a nuanced understanding of how ethical theories translate into real-world applications.

Consider the development of autonomous vehicles, a prime example where ethical theories must be meticulously applied to real-world technology. Engineers and developers face the daunting task of programming decision-making processes that align with ethical principles like minimizing harm and ensuring fairness. For instance, how should an autonomous vehicle react in an unavoidable accident scenario? Should it prioritize the safety of pedestrians, its passengers, or both? These are not just theoretical questions but vital considerations that must be addressed through complex algorithms and ethical reasoning. Integrating ethics into this technology involves a multidisciplinary approach, combining insights from ethics, engineering, and data science to create systems that comply with safety regulations and adhere to broader ethical standards.

However, translating these ethical theories into practice is fraught with challenges. One significant hurdle is the alignment of ethical AI development with commercial goals. In a market-driven economy, there is often a push to fast-track development cycles and minimize costs, which can lead to compromises in ethical rigor. Additionally, the inherently probabilistic nature of many AI systems introduces unpredictability in outcomes, making it difficult to ensure consistent ethical behavior. For example, AI models used in hiring may inadvertently learn and replicate biases present in historical hiring data, leading to unfair decision-making that contradicts ethical intentions despite developers' best efforts.

Despite these challenges, there are many success stories where ethical considerations have been effectively integrated into AI systems but have also driven their success. One notable example is the use of AI in healthcare, particularly in patient diagnosis and treatment plans. AI systems that adhere to ethical guidelines, ensuring patient confidentiality and informed consent, have significantly improved patient outcomes and efficiency in healthcare settings. These systems assist in diagnosing diseases from imaging data with a level of accuracy comparable to that of human experts, thereby enhancing the quality of care and patient trust in AI-enabled healthcare services.

Looking ahead, the role of ethics in AI is set to become increasingly influential as technology continues to evolve. Future developments in AI will likely see a greater emphasis on ethical AI design as public awareness of AI's ethical implications grows and regulatory bodies tighten standards. We can anticipate advancements in ethical AI audits, where systems are tested for efficiency and security but evaluated on ethical grounds to ensure they operate without bias and respect user privacy. Moreover, the rise of explainable AI and transparent systems will make aligning AI operations with ethical standards easier, fostering greater trust and cooperation between humans and machines.

As we advance into the age of artificial intelligence, the intersection of technology and ethics becomes more critical than ever. It is not merely about programming machines but about instilling values that uphold human dignity and societal well-being. The continuous evolution of AI ethics is not just a response to emerging technologies but a proactive approach to shaping a future where technology enhances the human experience without compromising moral integrity. As developers and ethicists, our role is to steer this evolution thoughtfully and responsibly, ensuring that as our machines learn, they do so in a way that reflects our highest ethical aspirations.

Chapter 2: Ethical Frameworks for AI Development

In artificial intelligence, the pace at which new advancements appear can often feel dizzying. Yet, amidst this rapid evolution, the steadfast pillar that must underlie these technologies is a robust ethical framework. Unlike the static laws of physics that govern the natural world, the principles that guide our interactions with AI are subject to cultural shifts, technological breakthroughs, and ever-expanding philosophical understandings. This chapter focuses on the scaffolding needed to build these frameworks—structures designed not only to withstand the pressures of today's challenges but also flexible enough to adapt to the unforeseen complexities of tomorrow.

2.1 Designing Actionable Ethical Frameworks for AI

Framework Fundamentals

At the core of any ethical framework for AI development are several non-negotiable components that guide their structure and implementation. First and foremost is the principle of beneficence, ensuring that AI technologies are designed primarily to benefit people and enhance human well-being. Supporting this is the principle of non-maleficence, which cautions against causing harm, whether through direct action or unintentional neglect. Another cornerstone is justice, which demands that AI technologies operate fairly and without bias, offering equal opportunity and consideration to all users. Finally, the principle of autonomy respects the right of individuals to make informed decisions about how AI technologies impact their lives. These components are not just abstract ideals; they are practical necessities that ensure AI technologies are developed with moral integrity and public accountability at their core.

Inclusivity and Diversity

The development of ethical frameworks must be an inclusive process that actively seeks and values diverse perspectives. This inclusivity is crucial not only from a moral standpoint but also for the practical efficacy of AI systems. Diverse teams are more likely to identify potential biases in AI design and better understand the varied contexts in which AI will operate. For instance, when AI technologies are used globally, frameworks developed with input from a culturally diverse group of ethicists, engineers, and end-users are more likely to be respected and adopted across different societies. This approach prevents the creation of homogeneous AI solutions that fail to address or even recognize the nuanced needs of diverse populations, thereby fostering technologies that are truly global in their design and compassionate in their application.

Adaptability

Given the dynamic nature of technology and ethics, ethical frameworks for AI must be inherently adaptable. They should be designed to evolve as new ethical challenges emerge and as our understanding of existing challenges deepens. This adaptability can be facilitated through periodic review processes, where frameworks are reassessed and revised in light of new information, technological advancements, or changes in societal values. For example, the rapid growth in the capabilities of machine learning models might necessitate updates in privacy protections or consent processes, ensuring that ethical standards keep pace with technological capabilities. Moreover, as AI systems increasingly interact with aspects of human life, the ethical frameworks governing their use must be flexible enough to address these expanding interfaces.

Implementation Challenges

Implementing ethical frameworks in AI development can encounter significant challenges despite the best intentions. One major hurdle is the translation of abstract ethical principles into concrete development practices. This often requires interdisciplinary collaboration that can be hindered by differing priorities and language barriers between fields. Additionally, stakeholders might be resistant to prioritizing speed and cost-efficiency over thorough ethical scrutiny. Overcoming these challenges requires a commitment to ethical education within AI teams, ensuring that all members understand the importance of ethics and are equipped to implement these principles in their work. It also necessitates strong leadership that champions ethical considerations as integral to designing and deploying AI technologies rather than as an afterthought.

Visual Element: Ethical Framework Components Infographic

Below is an infographic to help you understand and visualize the necessary components for a robust ethical AI framework. This visual tool dissects the critical principles of beneficence, non-maleficence, justice, and autonomy into actionable elements. It offers a clear overview of how these components interact and support one another in creating ethical AI systems.

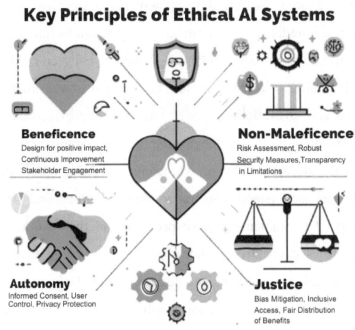

Figure 1 – Key Principles of Ethical AI

Understanding the principles of ethical AI:

1. **Beneficence:** This principle focuses on creating AI systems that promote the well-being of individuals and society. By designing for positive impact,

continuously improving AI, and engaging stakeholders, we can ensure AI applications enhance the quality of life and productivity.

   a. **Design for Positive Impact:** Ensure AI applications aim to improve quality of life, enhance productivity, and contribute positively to society.

   b. **Continuous Improvement:** Regularly update and refine AI systems to maximize benefits.

   c. **Stakeholder Engagement:** Involve diverse stakeholders in the development process to ensure the AI meets real-world needs.

2. **Non-Maleficence:** To avoid causing harm, it's crucial to conduct thorough risk assessments, implement robust security measures, and maintain transparency about AI systems' limitations and potential risks. This safeguards individuals and society from possible negative impacts.

   a. **Risk Assessment:** Conduct thorough risk assessments to identify potential harms.

   b. **Robust Security Measures:** Implement strong security protocols to protect against misuse and breaches.

c. **Transparency in Limitations:** Clearly communicate AI systems' limitations and potential risks.

3. **Justice:** Ensuring fair and equitable treatment in AI involves bias mitigation, inclusive access, and fair distribution of benefits. By addressing these elements, AI systems can be designed to be accessible and beneficial to all, including marginalized communities.

   a. **Bias Mitigation:** Implement strategies to detect and reduce biases in AI algorithms.

   b. **Inclusive Access:** Ensure AI technologies are accessible to all segments of society, including marginalized communities.

   c. **Fair Distribution of Benefits:** Ensure that the benefits of AI are distributed relatively across different groups.

4. **Autonomy:** Respecting individual rights in AI usage means providing informed consent, user control, and strong privacy protection. These elements ensure users understand and can control their interactions with AI systems, safeguarding their personal information.

a. **Informed Consent:** Provide clear information to users about how AI systems work and obtain their consent before use.

b. **User Control:** Design AI systems that allow users to understand, control quickly, and opt out if necessary.

c. **Privacy Protection:** Ensure robust data privacy measures to protect users' personal information.

Interaction and Support:

5. **Symbols:** Interlocking gears icon
6. **Synergy Between Principles:** Illustrate how these principles work together to create a balanced and ethical AI system.

   a. **Beneficence and Non-Maleficence:** Show that maximizing benefits (beneficence) while minimizing harm (non-maleficence) ensures AI systems are safe and effective.

   b. **Justice and Autonomy:** Explain that fair treatment (justice) and respect for user choices (autonomy) are critical for maintaining public trust and acceptance.

7. **Feedback Loop:** Demonstrates how continuous feedback and improvement help maintain ethical standards over time.

By internalizing these foundational elements, embracing inclusivity and diversity, committing to adaptability, and addressing implementation challenges head-on, you are equipped to construct ethical frameworks that guide current AI developments and flexibly adapt to future technological landscapes. This approach ensures that AI technologies stay aligned with human values and ethical standards, fostering a tech-enhanced world that respects and uplifts all individuals.

2.2 Case Studies: Ethical Frameworks in Action

In the intricate mesh of modern AI applications, ethical frameworks do not merely serve as theoretical constructs but as practical guides that shape real-world technology. These frameworks become particularly vital in sectors where AI's impact is profound and directly intersects with human rights and welfare, such as healthcare, autonomous vehicles, employment, and global initiatives. By examining how these frameworks function within varied contexts, we can glean insights into their practical utility and the nuanced challenges they address.

AI technologies promise revolutionary changes in healthcare, especially in diagnostics, patient monitoring, and personalized medicine. However, these advancements bring serious ethical considerations concerning patient privacy, informed consent, and fairness. For instance, AI systems that process sensitive health data must adhere strictly to privacy regulations such as HIPAA in the United States and GDPR in Europe. Ethical frameworks in this realm ensure that AI tools comply with these laws, but they also go further by embedding principles that safeguard patient confidentiality beyond mere legal requirements. Moreover, in the sphere of informed consent, these frameworks guide the development of transparent AI systems about their functionality and the extent of data usage, ensuring that patients understand what they consent to when they agree to the use of AI-driven treatments or diagnostics. This transparency is crucial for legal compliance and maintaining trust between healthcare providers and patients.

Additionally, fairness comes into play when considering how AI tools can provide equitable health outcomes across diverse patient groups. Ethical frameworks guide algorithms to avoid biases affecting diagnosis or treatment recommendations based on age, gender, race, or socioeconomic status. For example, AI-driven diagnostic tools are trained and regularly updated on diverse datasets to ensure they perform equally well across different demographics, thus upholding the ethical principle of fairness in medical treatment.

Turning our attention to autonomous vehicles (AVs), the ethical stakes involve life-and-death decisions, making the role of ethical frameworks exceptionally critical. These frameworks influence how AVs' decision-making algorithms are designed, mainly how they handle unavoidable accident scenarios, often discussed in the context of the 'trolley problem.'

As previously mentioned, the trolley problem is a thought experiment in ethics and moral philosophy. It explores the implications of making difficult moral choices and their guiding principles. The classic version of the problem is as follows:

A trolley is headed down a track towards five people who are tied up on the track and unable to move. You are standing next to a lever that can divert the trolley onto another track with one person tied up. You have two options:

1. Do nothing and allow the trolley to kill the five people.
2. Pull the lever, diverting the trolley onto the other track, where it will kill one person.

The trolley problem raises questions about utilitarianism (the idea that actions should be chosen based on their consequences and the goal of maximizing overall happiness) versus deontological ethics (the notion that actions should be judged based on their adherence to rules or duties, regardless of the consequences). It challenges individuals to consider whether it is morally permissible to sacrifice one life to save many others and whether causing harm (pulling the lever) is ethically different from allowing harm to occur through inaction.

Ethical frameworks help set up guidelines prioritizing human life and safety and ensuring compliance with traffic laws. For instance, in the development of AV software, moral principles are programmed into the decision-making algorithms to minimize harm under all circumstances, following the ethical principle of non-maleficence. These frameworks also ensure that AVs operate transparently and can explain decision-making processes to regulators and the public, fostering trust and acceptance. Moreover, fairness is addressed by ensuring that the algorithms do not discriminate against or favor specific individuals or groups when making split-second decisions. Regular ethical audits are conducted to assess and fine-tune these algorithms, ensuring their alignment with evolving ethical standards and technological advancements.

AI's role in hiring practices has been under increasing scrutiny in the employment sector. Ethical frameworks here focus on ensuring that AI-driven hiring tools do not perpetuate existing biases and operate with high transparency. For example, AI systems used in resume screening and candidate shortlisting are designed to disregard demographic factors like race, gender, and age, focusing solely on skills and qualifications relevant to the job. However, it has been noted that biases happen even with measures in place. For example, older workers were never taught how to cater their resumes for AI filters, so they are weeded out due to formatting and keyword mismatch, leading to more experienced workers having difficulty successfully modifying their resumes to be recognized by the AI tools.

The frameworks should enforce regular checks and balances, including algorithm audits and feedback loops, to identify and mitigate any emergent biases or discrepancies in evaluating candidates. More transparency in AI hiring tools involves clear communications to employers and candidates about how decisions are made, which factors are considered, and how data is handled. This ensures all parties are informed, and the process remains fair and just.

Lastly, global AI initiatives often require creating and adhering to comprehensive ethical frameworks that accommodate various cultural values and legal standards. These frameworks are crucial in projects spanning multiple countries, where varying norms and regulations could lead to moral conflicts. An example is the development of international AI-driven environmental monitoring systems, where data sharing and privacy must be managed across different jurisdictions. Ethical frameworks ensure that such projects uphold global equity in data access and benefits, respect local data protection laws, and maintain transparency about data usage and project goals. International collaborations, such as those under the auspices of the United Nations or other multinational organizations, often lead to developing these frameworks, ensuring that AI technologies are used responsibly and beneficially on a global scale.

These case studies show that ethical frameworks are not static rules but dynamic tools that adapt to the specific moral demands of various AI applications. They are crucial for ensuring that AI technologies serve humanity with fairness, transparency, and respect for individual rights, aligning technological advancements with our highest ethical aspirations.

2.3 Implementing Ethical Frameworks: A Step-by-Step Guide

The meticulous incorporation of ethical frameworks into AI development is not merely an academic exercise but a pragmatic process that requires careful planning, execution, and continuous refinement. The success of these frameworks hinges on their effective implementation, which is a multifaceted endeavor. This guide is a roadmap detailing each critical step from initial assessment to continuous improvement, ensuring that ethical considerations are deeply embedded within AI systems and practices.

Initial Assessment

The first step in implementing any ethical framework is thoroughly assessing existing practices. This crucial phase involves a comprehensive review of current AI technologies and processes to identify specific areas where ethical guidelines can be integrated. You, as developers and project managers, must scrutinize each component of your AI systems—from data collection and processing to algorithm design and output analysis—to pinpoint potential ethical vulnerabilities.

For example, if an AI application involves data that could potentially expose sensitive information, it is imperative to assess how this data is being safeguarded against misuse and whether privacy protections are adequate. Similarly, algorithms should be evaluated for any inherent biases that might affect their decisions, ensuring they align with the ethical principles of fairness and justice. This initial assessment not only helps in identifying the immediate adjustments needed but also lays the groundwork for integrating more comprehensive ethical considerations into the AI development lifecycle.

Stakeholder Engagement

Once the areas for ethical enhancement have been identified, the next step involves engaging all relevant stakeholders in the development and implementation of the ethical frameworks. This includes not just the AI developers and ethicists but also end-users, regulatory bodies, and potentially affected communities. Engaging a broad spectrum of stakeholders ensures that diverse viewpoints and concerns are considered, leading to more robust and inclusive ethical frameworks. For example, involving end-users in the development of an AI-driven health diagnostic tool can provide insights into patient privacy concerns and expectations, which might not be apparent to developers or ethicists alone. Similarly, regulatory bodies can offer guidance on compliance with existing laws and standards, which is crucial for the successful implementation of any AI technology. Effective stakeholder engagement is facilitated through regular meetings, workshops, and feedback sessions, creating a collaborative environment where ethical AI development is viewed as a shared responsibility.

Monitoring and Evaluation

With stakeholders engaged and ethical frameworks in place, the focus shifts to the ongoing monitoring and evaluation of these frameworks. This dynamic process involves not just tracking the compliance of AI systems with ethical guidelines but also assessing the real-world impact of these systems on users and society at large. Monitoring techniques might include periodic audits of AI systems, user feedback surveys, and metrics to assess algorithmic fairness and transparency.

Evaluation, on the other hand, involves a deeper analysis of the collected data to determine the effectiveness of the ethical frameworks in mitigating risks and enhancing the ethical operation of AI systems. For instance, if an AI application in financial services shows a disproportionate denial of loans to a particular demographic group, it would trigger an evaluation of the fairness protocols in place, prompting necessary adjustments. Regular monitoring and evaluation not only help in ensuring continuous compliance with ethical standards but also provide insights into how these standards can be improved.

Continuous Improvement

The final step in implementing ethical frameworks is perhaps the most critical—continuous improvement. The field of AI is characterized by rapid technological changes and evolving societal values, both of which can render existing ethical frameworks obsolete. Continuous improvement involves regularly updating ethical guidelines to accommodate new developments and insights. This could mean revising data privacy measures in response to new cybersecurity threats or updating fairness algorithms to reflect the latest research on bias mitigation. It requires a proactive approach, where potential ethical issues are anticipated and addressed before they manifest in AI systems. Continuous improvement ensures that ethical frameworks remain relevant and effective, adapting to new challenges and technologies as they arise.

In navigating these steps, you move beyond the theoretical underpinnings of ethical AI and engage with its practical realities. This process is not linear but cyclical, with each step informing and refining the others, creating a robust mechanism for ethical diligence in AI development. Through rigorous assessment, inclusive stakeholder engagement, vigilant monitoring, and committed continuous improvement, ethical frameworks do not just guide AI development but shape it to reflect our highest moral aspirations.

In wrapping up this chapter, we see that the journey of integrating ethics into AI is intricate and ongoing. The frameworks and strategies discussed here are not merely guidelines but tools for fostering a culture of responsibility in AI development. As we transition to the next chapter, the focus will shift from implementation strategies to specific ethical challenges and dilemmas faced in contemporary AI projects, where these frameworks will be tested. The lessons and methodologies outlined here will serve as a foundation for addressing these challenges, ensuring that AI continues to advance in a manner that is not only innovative but also conscientious and human-centric.

Chapter 3: Addressing Common Pain Points in AI Ethics

Navigating the ethical landscape of artificial intelligence is a significant and empowering task. It often feels like finding a path through a thick, uncharted forest. As developers and ethicists, you are at the forefront of pioneering this terrain, armed with the tools of technology and guided by the compass of moral philosophy. The complexities of AI ethics are not merely academic puzzles; they are real challenges that profoundly impact AI technologies' development, deployment, reception, and use. This chapter delves into some of the most pressing ethical conundrums you face. It offers strategies to navigate these effectively, ensuring your work advances technologically and aligns with the highest standards of ethical integrity. Remember, continuous education and active engagement in ethical debates are key to staying informed and up-to-date in this rapidly evolving field.

3.1 Navigating the Complexity of AI Ethics

The ethical landscape of AI is complex and demands a multidisciplinary approach. As you develop AI technologies, remember that these are not just technical projects but endeavors at the intersection of technology, ethics, law, and societal impact. A multidisciplinary approach, which brings together experts from various fields, such as computer science, philosophy, social sciences, and law, is crucial. This collaboration enriches the ethical analysis and ensures that diverse perspectives are considered, leading to more robust and inclusive AI solutions. For instance, while a computer scientist can design an algorithm to optimize efficiency, a social scientist might highlight potential societal impacts that require adjustments to the algorithm to prevent unintended consequences, such as discrimination or social exclusion.

Ethical dilemmas in AI are often complex and multifaceted, making them difficult to identify and articulate. Developing methodologies for clarifying these dilemmas is crucial. One effective method is using ethical decision-making frameworks. These frameworks guide you through a structured process of identifying ethical issues, considering the consequences of different actions, and making informed decisions. Tools such as ethical flowcharts or decision trees can help break down a dilemma into manageable parts, making evaluating the implications of various choices easier. For example, when faced with a decision about whether to implement a certain feature in an AI system that could potentially compromise user privacy, an ethical decision-making tree would help evaluate the trade-offs between technological benefits and ethical risks, guiding you to a decision that upholds your commitment to user rights and privacy.

Building trust and facilitating consensus is crucial in balancing conflicting interests in AI development. Stakeholders often have diverse and sometimes opposing priorities and values, which can lead to conflicts that are difficult to resolve. Strategies for balancing these interests involve open communication, transparency, and negotiation. Establishing clear channels for stakeholder engagement and feedback is essential. This could mean regular meetings with stakeholders to discuss ethical considerations and gather diverse inputs or public forums where broader community concerns can be addressed. Additionally, transparency about how decisions are made and whose interests are prioritized can build trust and facilitate consensus. For instance, if a decision is made to prioritize user privacy over some aspects of system functionality, explaining the ethical reasoning behind this decision can help stakeholders understand and support this choice.

To aid in these ethical decisions, various models and frameworks can be utilized. Ethical decision-making models, such as consequentialism, deontology, and virtue ethics, provide different lenses to view ethical dilemmas. These models can be applied individually or in combination to explore different dimensions of a dilemma, offering a more comprehensive understanding of the ethical landscape. For example, when developing AI for healthcare, consequentialist models can help assess the potential benefits and harms of the AI system, deontological models can ensure that the system complies with medical ethics and legal requirements, and virtue ethics can guide the development of AI systems that are compassionate and promote patient welfare.

Visual Element: Ethical Decision-Making Flowchart

The following flowchart outlines a fundamental process for navigating ethical dilemmas to facilitate further the understanding and application of ethical decision-making in AI. This tool guides you through the initial identification of the dilemma, various ethical assessments, and considerations, leading to a decision informed by multiple ethical perspectives.

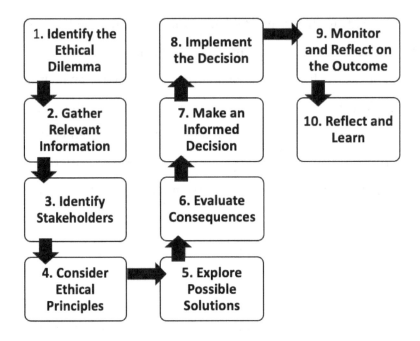

Figure 2 - Flowchart for Ethical Decision-Making

Everyone does not share the same core principles, but we all want to do the right thing, even when we are still determining what that might be. The flowchart is provided as a suggested methodology for exploring ethical dilemmas and identifying courses of action in AI decision-making processes. It guides you through some of the following steps:

1. **Identify the Ethical Dilemma:**

   Recognize the ethical issue at hand. For instance, if you are too closely or personally involved in the situation, or if other potential conflicts of interest exist, don't act immediately (even if a decision is urgent, pause briefly). Seek help*. Reach out to someone you trust for guidance. Assess if you need to recuse yourself.

2. Gather Relevant Information:

Collect all necessary facts and data about the situation. Get the facts - Not knowing all the information may be misleading.

3. Identify Stakeholders:

Not knowing all the information may be misleading. Who is involved, and who does it impact? Ensure your sources of information are accurate, and don't rely on secondhand information.

4. Consider Ethical Principles

Evaluate the situation using various ethical frameworks, such as utilitarianism, deontology, and virtue ethics. Review all Regulations, policies, and laws that might apply and keep them in mind as you think of solutions.

5. Explore Possible Solutions:

Which solution best addresses the situation while complying with the policies and laws identified? Does the proposed solution reflect the core values of AI ethics, such as fairness, transparency, and accountability? Is it honest? What are the likely negative and positive consequences of each solution? If the best approach is not straightforward, seek help. Reach out to someone to discuss. Generate and consider different courses of action.

6. Evaluate Consequences:

How would you feel if what you are about to do showed up on the front pages of the local newspaper, i.e., the front page test? Could you defend your actions? What would your response be if a decision made in private suddenly became public? By focusing on what others would think, this test can help prevent us from taking special advantage for ourselves, such as making excuses or unfairly justifying our actions. Assess the potential outcomes of each option, considering both short-term and long-term effects.

7. Make an Informed Decision:

Decide on the best solution. Take some time to think about how your decision can be communicated or implemented with the most outstanding care and attention to the concerns of all stakeholders. Acting with integrity sometimes takes courage. Based on your evaluation, choose the best ethical course of action.

8. Implement the decision:

Put the chosen solution into practice effectively.

9. Monitor and Reflect on the Outcome:

Observe the results of the decision and its impact on stakeholders. How did your decision turn out, and what have you learned from the specific situation that you can fall back in a similar situation next time?

10. Reflect and Learn:

Reflect on the decision-making process and outcomes to improve future ethical decision-making. You want to reach out to someone who will give you good advice, like a trusted advisor, a mentor, a colleague with integrity, or a subject matter expert.

This structured approach ensures that ethical considerations are thoroughly integrated into AI decision-making processes, helping to align technology with human values and ethical standards. By embracing a multidisciplinary approach, developing transparent methodologies for identifying and clarifying ethical dilemmas, employing strategies to balance conflicting interests, and utilizing various ethical decision-making models, you can navigate the complexities of AI ethics more effectively. These strategies help address the immediate ethical challenges and build a foundation for ethical integrity that enhances the credibility and societal acceptance of AI technologies. As you continue to engage with these complexities, remember that each ethical challenge you overcome not only solves a problem but also contributes to the broader goal of fostering an ethical culture in AI development, ensuring that as machines become more intelligent, our approach to their integration with society becomes wiser.

3.2 Staying Updated with Evolving Ethical Standards

In the rapidly evolving field of AI, staying informed about the latest ethical standards and regulations is not just beneficial—it's imperative for responsible AI development. As you navigate this dynamic landscape, leveraging professional networks can be crucial. Professional associations and networks dedicated to AI and ethics provide a platform for exchanging ideas, sharing best practices, and disseminating new research findings. These networks often organize conferences, webinars, and panel discussions that bring together leading experts in the field. Engaging with these platforms allows you to stay at the forefront of ethical AI development. For instance, joining groups such as the Association for the Advancement of Artificial Intelligence (AAAI) or the IEEE Standards Association can provide access to a wealth of resources and expert insights to guide your ethical decision-making processes. These associations often publish guidelines and white papers to help clarify complex ethical issues and offer direction on handling emerging ethical challenges.

Continuing education plays a pivotal role in ensuring that AI professionals like you remain well-informed about AI's latest advancements and ethical considerations. Workshops, courses, and seminars designed explicitly around AI ethics are becoming increasingly common in educational institutions and professional development platforms. These educational offerings are designed to keep you updated on technological advancements and the evolving landscape of AI ethics. They cover various topics, from privacy and data protection to fairness and transparency in AI algorithms. Engaging in these continuous learning opportunities ensures that you not only keep pace with technological advances but also deepen your understanding of the ethical implications of these technologies. For example, courses that offer case studies on real-world AI applications allow you to explore how ethical theories are applied in practice, enhancing your ability to implement these concepts in your work.

Regulatory compliance is another critical area where staying updated is essential. The legal landscape governing AI is continually changing, with new regulations and guidelines being developed both at national and international levels. Understanding and complying with these regulations is crucial not only for legal adherence but also for ethical integrity. For instance, the European Union's General Data Protection Regulation (GDPR) has set significant precedents in how personal data is handled by AI systems, impacting AI projects globally. Staying informed about such regulations ensures that your AI projects meet legal standards and uphold high ethical standards. Regularly reviewing updates from regulatory bodies, participating in compliance workshops, and consulting with legal experts in AI ethics can help you navigate this complex regulatory environment. This proactive approach mitigates the risk of legal repercussions and builds trust with users and stakeholders by demonstrating a commitment to ethical compliance.

Finally, active engagement with ongoing ethical debates and research in the field of AI is essential for staying informed and influential in shaping the future of AI ethics. The field of AI ethics is vibrant, with scholarly articles, ethical debates, and new research findings continually challenging and advancing our understanding of ethical AI. Engaging with this academic and professional discourse through reading, contributing to discussions, and conducting your research can provide deeper insights into ethical issues and how they evolve with AI advancements. Participation in forums, ethical review boards, and public debates about AI ethics keeps you informed and allows you to contribute to developing ethical standards and practices in AI. This active involvement ensures that you are not just a consumer of ethical guidelines but also a contributor to the ethical discourse, playing a role in shaping the standards that will govern future AI development.

Navigating the complexities of AI ethics requires a proactive and informed approach involving continuous learning, engagement with professional networks, strict adherence to regulations, and active participation in ethical debates. By embracing these strategies, you ensure that your work in AI advances technologically and does so with a firm ethical foundation, effectively addressing the challenges posed by this dynamic field.

3.3 Bias and Fairness: From Identification to Mitigation

In the field of artificial intelligence, ensuring fairness and mitigating bias represent pivotal challenges that directly impact the effectiveness and ethical integrity of AI systems. As developers, it's crucial to adopt rigorous methods for identifying and addressing bias, which can often infiltrate AI algorithms and datasets, sometimes subtly. Bias in AI can manifest in various forms, from data that reflects historical inequalities to algorithms that propagate these biases further. To combat this, a structured approach to identifying these biases is necessary. Techniques such as sensitivity analysis, which examines how changes in input data affect AI outputs, and disparity impact analysis, which evaluates the outcomes of AI decisions across different demographic groups, are invaluable. These methods help illuminate biases that may not be immediately apparent, ensuring that AI systems perform equitably across diverse user groups.

Once biases have been identified, the next step involves implementing strategies to mitigate these biases effectively. This process begins at the data level, ensuring diversity and representativeness in the datasets used to train AI models. Techniques such as re-sampling the data to balance representation or applying algorithmic corrections to adjust biased data distributions are often employed. Beyond data manipulation, bias can also be mitigated at the algorithmic level through the development of fairness-aware algorithms. These algorithms are designed to make decisions that account for fairness explicitly, often by including fairness constraints or objectives during the learning process. Regular testing and validation against bias are also crucial—this involves continuously monitoring the AI system's decisions to ensure they remain free from bias post-deployment, adapting the system as necessary when new forms of bias are detected.

The role of fairness metrics in this process cannot be overstated. These metrics provide quantifiable means to assess the fairness of AI systems. Common fairness metrics include demographic parity, which requires that decisions be independent of sensitive attributes like race or gender; equality of opportunity, which ensures that all groups have equal accurate positive rates; and individual fairness, which mandates that similar individuals receive similar treatments. Each metric offers different perspectives on fairness, and often, the choice of metric must align with the specific ethical goals of the AI application. Understanding the implications of each metric and choosing appropriately based on the context is crucial for effectively managing fairness in AI systems.

To bring these concepts to life, let's consider real-world applications where bias identification and mitigation have been successfully implemented. A significant financial institution employed AI to improve loan approval processes in one notable instance. Initially, the AI model inadvertently favored applicants from specific zip codes. The bias was identified through sensitivity analysis, which led to re-evaluating and expanding the training datasets to include a broader range of socio-economic demographics. Fairness-aware algorithms were developed to ensure that loan approvals adhered to equality of opportunity, significantly reducing bias in loan distributions. Another example involves a tech company that developed a hiring algorithm that exhibited gender bias, favoring male candidates over equally qualified female candidates. The company used disparity impact analysis to identify this bias and implemented algorithmic adjustments that ensured gender parity in candidate selection. These cases exemplify the practical challenges and solutions in bias mitigation, highlighting the ongoing need for vigilance and adaptability in managing AI ethics.

As we conclude this exploration of bias and fairness in AI, it becomes evident that these are not just technical issues but fundamentally ethical ones that affect real lives and societal structures. The methodologies and case studies discussed here underscore the necessity for a proactive approach to ethical AI development that continuously strives for fairness and actively counters bias. By integrating these practices into your AI projects, you contribute not only to the advancement of technology but also to the fostering of a more just and equitable society.

The next chapter will delve into the ethical considerations surrounding data privacy and protection in AI, expanding on how these principles intersect with the broader goals of fairness and transparency in artificial intelligence. This discussion will further illuminate the interconnected nature of AI ethics, providing a comprehensive understanding of navigating these multifaceted challenges in your professional practice.

Chapter 4: Data Privacy and Protection

In an era where the nightly news reports on data breaches with unsettling frequency, the importance of embedding privacy into the DNA of artificial intelligence (AI) systems cannot be overstated. Imagine a world where AI optimizes our lifestyle and work processes by intrusively mining our personal information without explicit consent. The backlash from such scenarios underscores the critical need for Privacy by Design - a concept that, when ingrained in AI development, ensures the technology we trust is also the technology that respects our personal boundaries. This chapter delves into the foundational principles of Privacy by Design. It explores its technical implementations, ethical justifications, and real-world applications in AI projects, ensuring you are equipped to develop AI solutions that honor user privacy while delivering unparalleled functionality.

4.1 Constructing AI with Privacy by Design

Foundational Principles

Privacy by Design, a concept introduced by Dr. Ann Cavoukian, is based on the principle that ensuring privacy should be an organization's standard mode of operation.

Applied to AI, this concept translates into developing systems that integrate privacy considerations from the outset, not as an afterthought but as a foundational framework guiding all stages of AI development. The principles of Privacy by Design are universal, applicable across sectors and jurisdictions, and incredibly pertinent in the context of AI. They emphasize proactive measures, privacy as the default setting, end-to-end security, and visibility and transparency. Embracing these principles means designing AI systems that inherently protect user data by minimizing data usage, securing data throughout its lifecycle, and maintaining transparency about data practices.

Technical Implementation

The technical implementation of Privacy by Design in AI involves several strategic approaches. First and foremost, data protection should be embedded into the design of AI technologies. This can be achieved through techniques such as data minimization, where only the data necessary for a specific purpose is collected, and pseudonymization, where collected data is processed in a way that it cannot be attributed back to a specific user without additional information. Another crucial element is the implementation of robust encryption methods to safeguard data at rest and in transit, ensuring that the integrity and confidentiality of user data remain intact even in the event of unauthorized access. Moreover, AI systems must be designed to facilitate user access to their data, allowing them to review, modify, or delete their information as needed. Implementing these technical measures strengthens the privacy capabilities of AI systems and builds user trust, a crucial component in the widespread adoption of AI technologies.

Ethical Justification

The ethical justification for prioritizing privacy in AI development extends beyond compliance and risk management—it is fundamentally about respecting individual autonomy and dignity. In the context of AI, where decisions can be made automatically and at scale, maintaining privacy is crucial to protect individuals from potential harm, discrimination, or manipulation. Privacy by Design respects the user's right to control their personal information, an extension of their autonomy, and a reflection of their dignity. It also addresses broader societal concerns, such as the potential for surveillance and the erosion of individual freedoms, which can be mitigated by adopting strong privacy-preserving measures in AI systems. By prioritizing privacy, developers and organizations adhere to ethical standards and contribute to a societal framework where technology serves humanity without undermining fundamental rights.

Case Examples

Implementing Privacy by Design in AI is not theoretical; numerous organizations have successfully integrated these principles into their AI projects, demonstrating both feasibility and benefits. For instance, a European financial technology company developed an AI-driven personal finance advisor that uses machine learning to provide customized financial advice to users. From the outset, the project was designed to anonymize user data, ensuring that personal financial information was never stored or processed in an identifiable form. This complied with stringent European data protection standards and enhanced consumer trust, significantly contributing to the product's success in a competitive market.

Another example involves a healthcare AI startup that developed a diagnostic tool using patient data. By implementing Privacy by Design, the company ensured that all patient data was encrypted, minimal data was used for diagnostic purposes, and all data processing was transparent and accountable to both patients and regulators. This approach safeguarded patient privacy and aligned with ethical standards for medical practice, enhancing the tool's credibility and acceptance in the healthcare community.

Visual Element: Privacy by Design Framework Infographic

An infographic is provided below to encapsulate the core aspects of Privacy by Design and its application in AI. This visual representation highlights the seven foundational principles of Privacy by Design. It illustrates how they can be practically implemented in AI development, providing a quick reference that reinforces the importance of integrating these principles into every phase of AI projects.

Privacy by Design

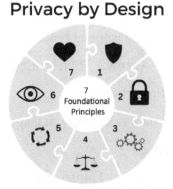

Figure 3 - Seven Fundamental Principles of Privacy by Design

Each icon in the diagram represents the essence of each one of the seven foundational principles of Privacy by Design:

1. **Shield**: Proactive, not Reactive; Preventative, not Remedial.
   - Focus on proactive measures to prevent privacy breaches.
2. **Lock**: Privacy as the Default Setting
   - Ensure that personal data is automatically protected.
3. **Embedded Gear**: Privacy Embedded into Design
   - Incorporate privacy considerations into the design and architecture of IT systems and business practices.
4. **Balancing Scale**: Full Functionality—Positive-Sum, not Zero-Sum
   - Avoid false dichotomies, such as privacy vs. security, and achieve both.
5. **Lifecycle Arrow**: End-to-End Security—Full Lifecycle Protection
   - Ensure data is securely managed from collection to deletion.
6. **Eye**: Visibility and Transparency

- Keep processes open and transparent to stakeholders.

7. **Heart**: Respect for User Privacy

- Keep user privacy interests paramount by offering strong privacy defaults, appropriate notice, and user-friendly options.

By thoroughly understanding and implementing the principles of Privacy by Design, you are equipped to protect user data and foster an environment where AI is used responsibly and ethically. This commitment to privacy enhances the functionality and acceptance of AI systems and aligns with a broader commitment to ethical standards and societal well-being. As AI continues to evolve and permeate various aspects of our lives, the principles discussed in this chapter provide a robust foundation for ensuring that our technological advancements continue to respect and protect our most fundamental values.

4.2 Ethical Data Collection and Usage

In the intricate web of modern AI development, the manner in which data is collected, used, and managed not only impacts the effectiveness of the AI systems but also significantly influences public trust and regulatory compliance. One of the foundational elements of ethical AI practice involves obtaining informed consent and ensuring transparency in data collection processes. Informed consent means that individuals are fully aware of and understand what data is being collected, why it is being collected, how it will be used, and who will have access to it before they agree to provide their personal information. This practice is not merely a legal formality but a fundamental respect for individual autonomy and a cornerstone of trust between technology developers and users. Transparency in this context involves clear communication about data collection practices and data usage purposes. This includes accessible privacy policies and regular updates to participants on how their data is being used, especially as AI systems evolve. For instance, when users interact with AI-driven platforms like digital assistants, they should be able to easily access information on what personal data the assistant collects and how it influences the functionality offered.

Moreover, the principle of data minimization plays a crucial role in ethical AI development. This principle advocates for the collection and use of only the data that is absolutely necessary for the specific purposes stated. Data minimization reduces the risk of harm in the event of a data breach by limiting the amount of data exposed. It also aligns with broader ethical principles by not collecting more information than is warranted, thus respecting users' privacy. In practice, applying data minimization involves scrutinizing the data requirements of AI systems during the design phase to ensure that only essential data elements are collected. For example, an AI application developed for personalized content recommendations should limit data collection to information directly relevant to content preferences and avoid irrelevant data that could lead to privacy infringements.

Anonymization techniques are another critical area in the ethical use of data. Anonymization involves altering personal data in such a way that the individual is not or is no longer identifiable. This process is crucial for protecting privacy, especially in contexts where the public sharing of data is involved, such as in academic research or public health studies. Techniques such as data masking, where specific identifiers are removed or altered, and differential privacy, which adds enough 'noise' to the data to prevent the identification of individuals while still allowing for valuable insights to be derived, are effective strategies for anonymization. These techniques enable researchers and developers to utilize large datasets for training and improving AI systems without compromising the personal privacy of the individuals whose data is included in these datasets.

However, these practices have their ethical challenges. The very collection and utilization of data by AI systems introduce several ethical concerns, including the potential for surveillance and exploitation. The capability of AI to analyze vast amounts of data can be leveraged to monitor individuals' behaviors and preferences at an unprecedented scale, raising concerns about surveillance and the erosion of privacy. For instance, AI systems employed in the workplace to monitor productivity can inadvertently lead to invasive surveillance practices that monitor much more than just work-related activities. Moreover, exploiting personal data, especially without transparent consent and ethical justification, can lead to manipulation and discrimination. AI systems that target individuals for digital advertising based on extensive personal profiling may exploit vulnerabilities or biases in human psychology for commercial gain, raising significant ethical concerns.

Navigating these challenges requires a careful balance between leveraging data for AI development and upholding ethical standards that protect individual rights and societal values. By adhering to principles of consent, transparency, data minimization, and employing robust anonymization techniques, you can ensure that your AI projects achieve technical excellence and respect and promote the ethical values essential to fostering trust and integrity in the age of artificial intelligence.

4.3 Global Data Privacy Laws and AI Compliance

Navigating the complex terrain of global data privacy laws is akin to steering through a labyrinth where new challenges and compliance requirements are introduced at each turn. As an AI developer, understanding the nuances of significant data protection regulations such as the General Data Protection Regulation (GDPR) in the European Union, the California Consumer Privacy Act (CCPA) in the United States, and other international frameworks is crucial. These laws have been crafted with specific goals and contexts, influencing AI development in unique ways.

The GDPR, for instance, is renowned for its stringent requirements and broad scope, impacting any business dealing with EU residents' data, regardless of the company's location. It emphasizes principles like data minimization, purpose limitation, and the rights of data subjects to access and control their personal information. These requirements necessitate that AI systems processing EU residents' data incorporate strong privacy protections and provide user data access and deletion mechanisms upon request. On the other hand, the CCPA focuses on providing consumers with the right to know about and opt out of the sale of their personal information, introducing a different set of compliance strategies, particularly around consumer communications and data handling practices.

Apart from GDPR and CCPA, other regions like Brazil, with its General Data Protection Law (LGPD), and China, with its Personal Information Protection Law (PIPL), have also introduced regulations that add layers to the compliance landscape. Each of these laws affects how data can be collected, stored, and used, requiring AI systems to be adaptable to various compliance environments. A comparative analysis of these laws shows a common trend towards greater transparency, enhanced data protection measures, and increased individual rights, guiding how AI must be designed and operated globally.

Navigating compliance with these diverse regulations requires a strategic approach where understanding local laws is just as important as grasping international standards. One effective strategy is implementing a universal data protection framework within your organization that meets the highest data privacy standards, such as those outlined in GDPR. This framework can then be adjusted as needed to meet additional local requirements. Regular training and updates for your AI development team on changes in data privacy laws are also vital, ensuring everyone is informed, and compliance is integrated into every stage of AI system development.

Cross-border data flows present another layer of complexity, especially when AI systems transfer personal data across geographical boundaries. Different countries have varying requirements for international data transfer; for instance, GDPR requires that data transferred out of the EU be handled according to standards that provide an equivalent level of protection. Managing these requirements often involves implementing legal mechanisms such as Standard Contractual Clauses (SCCs) or ensuring that the receiving country has an adequacy decision from the European Commission. Ethically, it is crucial to maintain the integrity and confidentiality of personal data throughout these processes, respecting the privacy rights of individuals across different jurisdictions.

Finally, staying agile and responsive to regulatory changes is crucial for maintaining compliance in a field as dynamic as AI. This can be achieved by proactively monitoring legislative developments and participating in industry forums and discussions that provide insights into upcoming regulations. Building flexible data governance frameworks that can quickly adapt to new laws and guidelines can help ensure that your AI systems remain compliant over time, regardless of how data privacy landscapes evolve.

In this intricate web of global data privacy laws and AI compliance, the overarching goal remains clear: to develop AI systems that push the boundaries of technological capabilities while respecting and protecting individual privacy and adhering to the highest legal compliance standards. This commitment enhances the credibility and acceptance of AI technologies and aligns with broader ethical considerations that are becoming increasingly central to technological advancements in the digital age.

As we conclude this exploration of data privacy and protection in AI, we are reminded of the delicate balance between innovation and individual rights. The principles and strategies discussed across these sections form a robust foundation for respecting user privacy and navigating the complex regulatory environments that govern AI development. Looking ahead, the next chapter will delve deeper into the ethical considerations surrounding bias and fairness in AI, building on our understanding of data protection to tackle issues of equality and justice in AI applications. This progression underscores the interconnected nature of AI ethics, where protecting data privacy is intricately linked with ensuring fairness and upholding justice in technological advancements.

Make a Difference with Your Review

Thanks to your feedback, support, and reviews, I'm able to create the best books possible and serve more people.

I would be extremely grateful if you could take just 60 seconds to leave an honest review of the book on Amazon kindly. Please share your feedback and thoughts for others to see.

To do so, scan the QR code to share your thoughts. Select a star rating and write a couple of sentences. That's it!

I'm excited to help you understand why Artificial Intelligence Ethics is so important, as more and more of our lives are made better by using AI. Thank you from the bottom of my heart.

Now, let's dive back into our exciting journey.

Debbie Sue Jancis

Chapter 5: Bias and Fairness in AI

Imagine you are designing a garden, meticulously selecting plants, arranging them, and ensuring each has just what it needs to thrive—light, space, nutrients. However, without realizing it, you've planted so that some plants shadow others, causing uneven growth. This unintentional oversight in gardening can illustrate how biases, often unrecognized, can permeate AI systems, affecting their fairness and effectiveness. In the realm of artificial intelligence, biases can distort AI behavior, leading to decisions that might systematically favor one group over another. As you delve deeper into the world of AI development, understanding these biases, identifying their sources, and mitigating their impact becomes crucial. This chapter will guide you through the nuances of identifying and assessing bias in AI models, ensuring your AI systems grow as intended, fair, and unbiased.

5.1 Identifying Bias in AI Models

Sources of Bias

Bias in AI can originate from multiple sources throughout the lifecycle of data handling and model development.

Initially, bias can seep in during data collection. This stage is critical as the data is the foundational bedrock on which AI models are built. For example, if an AI model is trained on historical hiring data to screen job applicants, and if historically the data reflects a preference for a specific demographic, the AI could inadvertently learn to replicate these biases. Similarly, bias can come from how data is labeled, which is often a subjective process influenced by the labeler's perspectives and experiences. Another profound source is the algorithmic design itself. Algorithms, despite being mathematical, do not operate in a vacuum; they are crafted by humans who may, even unintentionally, embed their conscious or unconscious biases into algorithmic choices and model parameters.

Detection Tools

To identify these biases, several sophisticated tools and methodologies have been developed. Statistical tests, for instance, can be employed to analyze whether the outcomes of an AI model systematically differ across groups defined by variables such as age, gender, or ethnicity. Another powerful tool is 'adversarial testing,' where the model is subjected to various challenging scenarios to uncover hidden biases. Machine learning fairness toolkits, like

Google's TensorFlow Fairness Indicators, offer a suite of metrics that help evaluate and compare model predictions across different user groups. These tools are essential in the early detection of biases, allowing developers like you to take corrective measures before the model is deployed.

Impact Assessment

Understanding the potential impact of bias in AI models is paramount. This involves not just recognizing that biases exist but evaluating how they affect different populations. Impact assessments are essential in fields where decisions have significant repercussions, such as healthcare, criminal justice, and employment. For instance, a biased AI model in healthcare could lead to poorer health outcomes for underrepresented groups by failing to accurately diagnose conditions that manifest differently across populations. Therefore, conducting thorough impact assessments helps understand the broader implications of AI biases, guiding developers to implement more equitable AI systems.

Bias in Model Interpretation

Moreover, biases can also emerge in how end-users interpret the outputs of AI models. Even if an AI model is technically unbiased, how its results are used and interpreted can introduce bias. For example, if a predictive policing tool disproportionately flags specific neighborhoods as high risk, it could lead to increased surveillance of those areas, perpetuating a cycle of over-policing, regardless of the actual crime rate. Thus, as AI developers, you must consider the construction of AI models and their application, ensuring that interpretations do not reinforce existing prejudices.

Visual Element: Bias Identification and Impact Assessment Flowchart

Below is a flowchart that outlines a step-by-step process for detecting biases and evaluating their impacts to aid in the systematic identification and assessment of bias within AI models. This tool serves as a practical guide in your efforts to develop fair and unbiased AI systems.

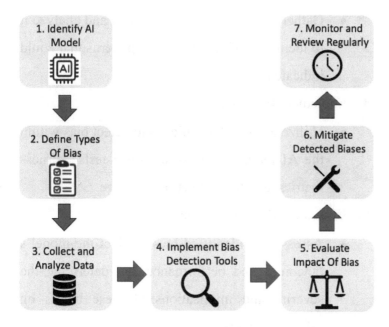

Figure 4 - Flowchart for Detecting Biases and Evaluating Their Impacts in AI Models

1. **Identify AI Model:**
   - Recognize the AI model in use and understand its purpose and functionality.
2. **Define Types of Bias**
   - Specify the different types of biases that may be relevant (e.g., data bias, algorithm bias, user bias).
3. **Collect and Analyze Data**

- Gather data used by the AI model and analyze it to identify any imbalances or patterns that could indicate bias.

4. Implement Bias Detection Tools
   - Utilize tools and techniques to detect bias within the AI model, such as statistical tests, fairness metrics, and bias detection software.

5. Evaluate the Impact of Bias
   - Assess how identified biases affect the model's outcomes and performance and determine the severity and implications of these biases on different groups.

6. Mitigate Detected Bias
   - Develop and implement strategies to mitigate or eliminate identified biases, such as data preprocessing, adjusting algorithms, or retraining the model with more balanced data.

7. Monitor and Review Regularly
   - Continuously monitor the AI model for any new biases that may arise and regularly review and update the model to ensure ongoing fairness and unbiased performance.

By rigorously identifying the sources of bias, utilizing advanced detection tools, assessing the potential impacts, and considering the implications of model interpretation, you are better equipped to cultivate AI systems that are not only intelligent but also just and fair. As you navigate the complex landscape of AI development, keep these considerations at the forefront of your work, ensuring that your technological creations serve all sections of society equitably.

5.2 Strategies for Mitigating AI Bias

In the continuous effort to refine AI technologies, ensuring the diversity of the datasets used during the training phase is a fundamental strategy for counteracting bias. Consider the diverse world these models will serve as you develop AI models. Incorporating a broad spectrum of data that reflects varied demographics, including age, ethnicity, gender, socioeconomic status, and more, is crucial. This diversity in data helps prevent the model from developing skewed understandings and biases that can occur when trained predominantly on homogenous datasets. For instance, when training facial recognition systems, using a dataset with a wide array of ethnic backgrounds can significantly reduce racial biases, ensuring the model performs accurately across different demographics. Moreover, diversity in datasets enhances the fairness of the AI applications and improves their robustness and generalizability, making them more adaptable to varied real-world scenarios. By prioritizing the assembly of diverse datasets, you advocate for equity in AI outputs and enhance the overall performance of the models, truly capturing the essence of global inclusivity.

Another critical measure in mitigating bias involves conducting thorough algorithmic audits. These audits are meticulous processes that examine the decisions made by AI systems to ensure they are free of bias. Think of these audits as a detailed inspection of a machine's workings, akin to a car's engine check-up, ensuring everything functions as intended without unintended noises or emissions. During an algorithmic audit, various aspects of the AI model are scrutinized, including the design of the algorithm, the decision-making processes, and the outcomes. The benefits of these audits are manifold. They identify and help rectify biases and bolster the AI systems' transparency, building trust among users and stakeholders. For example, an audit might reveal that an AI credit scoring system disproportionately disadvantages people from certain zip codes, prompting a recalibration of the model to correct this bias. Regularly scheduled audits, conducted by internal or external experts, ensure ongoing accountability and integrity in AI operations, instilling a layer of systematic scrutiny that upholds ethical standards and user confidence.

Inclusive design practices represent another cornerstone in crafting unbiased AI systems. These practices emphasize the involvement of a diverse group of stakeholders at every stage of AI development. From the initial design phase to testing and deployment, including voices from varied backgrounds, especially those often underrepresented in tech, ensures a multitude of perspectives are considered, enhancing the system's inclusivity. This approach is particularly effective in preemptively identifying potential biases that might not be evident to a more homogenous team. For instance, involving stakeholders from different cultural backgrounds can provide insights into locale-specific nuances that might affect the AI's functionality in those regions. Engaging with a broad base of perspectives enriches the development process. It aligns the end product more closely with a global user base's diverse needs and values, fostering a deeper connection and relevance of the technology in people's lives.

Lastly, the significance of ongoing monitoring of AI systems post-deployment cannot be overstated. Continuous monitoring safeguards against emerging biases, ensuring that AI systems remain fair and equitable throughout their operational lifecycle. As societal norms and values evolve, so too can the manifestations of bias within AI systems. Continuous monitoring involves regularly assessing the performance of AI applications to detect any deviations from expected ethical standards. This proactive surveillance allows for timely AI system adjustments, maintaining alignment with ethical norms and societal expectations. For example, an AI-driven job recommendation engine might initially perform without bias, but new biases could emerge as the job market evolves. Ongoing monitoring enables the identification of these shifts, allowing for modifications to the AI algorithms that realign with the current ethical and societal framework. This relentless pursuit of integrity in AI systems through continuous monitoring ensures compliance with evolving standards and reinforces the commitment to fairness and reliability in AI technologies.

By implementing these strategic measures, ensuring diversity in training datasets, conducting rigorous algorithmic audits, practicing inclusive design, and maintaining ongoing monitoring, you fortify the foundations of fairness in AI development. These strategies collectively function as a dynamic framework that addresses immediate biases and adapts to new challenges, continually steering AI technologies toward more ethical, unbiased, and equitable horizons.

5.3 Case Study: Overcoming Bias in AI Hiring Tools

In the dynamic field of AI development, the creation and implementation of hiring tools powered by artificial intelligence present unique challenges, especially concerning bias. These tools, designed to streamline recruitment by automating candidate screening and selection, can inadvertently perpetuate historical biases if not carefully managed. A notable case that sheds light on these challenges involved a well-known tech company that encountered significant setbacks when its AI hiring tool exhibited gender bias, favoring male candidates over females for technical roles.

The initial challenge was recognizing the bias, which was deeply embedded in the training algorithms. The AI system had been trained on historical employment data from the company, which, due to existing disparities in the tech industry, included significantly more men than women in technical roles. The AI, learning from this data, erroneously inferred that being male was a favorable trait for technical positions. This revelation came during routine performance evaluations of the tool, highlighting the critical need for vigilant oversight in AI tools handling sensitive tasks like hiring.

To tackle this issue, the company embarked on a series of strategic interventions aimed at identifying and mitigating the embedded biases. The first step involved revising the dataset used for training the AI. This revision meant not only expanding the data pool to include a more balanced representation of genders across technical roles but also applying techniques to anonymize candidates' demographic information, ensuring the AI focused on skills and qualifications rather than gender. Additionally, the development team implemented a modified algorithm designed to check and counteract any skewness towards a particular demographic, a technique known as 'fairness through awareness,' which explicitly adjusts decisions to achieve fairness.

The outcomes of these mitigation strategies were profoundly positive. The retrained AI hiring tool demonstrated a marked improvement in gender parity in candidate selection, aligning closely with the company's commitment to diversity and inclusion. Furthermore, the case study was a crucial learning experience for the organization, highlighting the importance of ongoing monitoring and evaluation of AI systems. It highlighted the necessity of having robust mechanisms in place to detect and correct biases that may arise as the external environment and internal data landscapes evolve.

Based on the insights gained from this case study, several guidelines can be proposed for ethically developing and implementing AI hiring tools. First, ensuring diversity in training datasets is crucial. This diversity should reflect not just gender but a broad spectrum of demographic and cultural backgrounds to safeguard against multifaceted biases. Second, incorporating transparency by design in AI tools is essential. This means building systems where operations, especially decisions and the bases for these decisions, are visible and understandable to users, fostering trust and accountability. Third, it is advisable to establish a routine for the ethical audit of AI systems, a practice that examines not only the technical performance but also the ethical implications of AI outputs. Lastly, engaging stakeholders from various backgrounds in the development process can provide diverse perspectives that challenge normative biases and contribute to more equitable AI solutions.

5.4 Case Study: The Gender Shades Project

Introduction

The Gender Shades project, spearheaded by Joy Buolamwini, is a seminal study that investigates the accuracy of facial analysis algorithms across different demographic groups, particularly focusing on gender and skin tone. This research highlights the disparities in the performance of commercial AI systems and underscores the ethical implications of biased AI technologies.

Background

Joy Buolamwini, an AI researcher and founder of the Algorithmic Justice League, conducted the Gender Shades project as part of her graduate work at the MIT Media Lab. The project emerged from her personal experiences and observations of facial recognition systems failing to accurately detect her face due to her dark skin tone.

Objective

The primary objective of the Gender Shades project was to evaluate the performance of facial analysis algorithms across different gender and skin tone groups to reveal any biases and discrepancies. The study aimed to raise awareness about the ethical challenges posed by biased AI systems and advocate for more inclusive and fair AI development practices.

Methodology:

1. **Dataset Creation:**
   o The research utilized the Pilot Parliaments Benchmark (PPB) dataset, which comprised over 1,200 images of parliamentarians from Rwanda, Senegal, South Africa, Iceland, Finland, and Sweden.
   o The dataset was carefully curated to ensure a balanced representation across gender (male and female) and skin tone (using the Fitzpatrick skin type classification).

2. **Evaluation of Commercial AI Systems:**
   o The study assessed the performance of three leading commercial facial analysis systems from Microsoft, IBM, and Face++.

o   The evaluation focused on the accuracy of gender classification across different demographic groups.

3. **Analysis and Metrics:**

   o   The algorithms were tested for their ability to correctly classify the gender of individuals in the PPB dataset.

   o   Error rates were analyzed and compared across various demographic intersections, particularly focusing on gender and skin tone.

Key Findings:

1. **Accuracy Disparities:**

   o   The study revealed significant accuracy disparities in gender classification across different demographic groups.

   o   For lighter-skinned males, the error rate was relatively low (less than 1%).

   o   The error rates were significantly higher for darker-skinned females, with some systems exhibiting error rates as high as 34.7%.

2. **Bias in Commercial Systems:**

- All three commercial AI systems showed biases, with lower accuracy rates for darker-skinned individuals, especially women.
- The study highlighted the systemic issue of AI bias and the potential harm it can cause to marginalized groups.

Impact and Significance:

1. **Awareness and Advocacy:**
   - The Gender Shades project brought significant attention to the issue of bias in AI, sparking widespread discussions in both academic and public spheres.
   - It emphasized the need for diversity and inclusivity in AI development, data collection, and algorithm training processes.

2. **Industry Response:**
   - Following the publication of the Gender Shades study, companies like IBM and Microsoft committed to improving the fairness and accuracy of their facial analysis algorithms.
   - The project increased scrutiny of AI systems and prompted many organizations to adopt

more rigorous bias detection and mitigation strategies.

3. **Ongoing Research and Policy:**
    o The findings of the Gender Shades project have influenced further research into algorithmic fairness and have informed policy discussions on AI ethics and regulation.
    o The project has inspired other researchers and advocates to explore and address biases in various AI applications.

The Gender Shades project is a landmark study that exposed the biases in facial analysis technologies and highlighted the ethical imperatives of developing fair and inclusive AI systems. By demonstrating the disparities in algorithmic performance across gender and skin tone, the project underscored the importance of diversity in AI research and the need for continuous efforts to eliminate technological biases.

Transitioning from the specific challenges and solutions of this case study to general practices, the next chapter will explore the broader ethical considerations in AI applications beyond hiring. This will include discussions on privacy, security, and the social implications of AI, ensuring a holistic approach to responsible AI development in various domains.

Chapter 6: AI and the Future of Work

As you delve into the intricacies of artificial intelligence and its role in the modern workplace, it's crucial to step back and consider a broader picture. In this landscape, AI is not merely a tool of convenience but a transformative force reshaping the fabric of employment and labor dynamics. Integrating AI into various sectors is not a distant future scenario; it is a present reality with profound implications for job displacement and creation. This chapter will guide you through a nuanced exploration of how AI impacts jobs across different industries, informed by economic theories, enriched with sector-specific analyses, and illustrated through insightful case studies. Additionally, we will address the critical issue of social equity, ensuring that AI's opportunities are accessible to all, paving the way for a more inclusive future.

6.1 AI's Impact on Job Displacement and Creation

Sector-Specific Analyses

The influence of AI on the labor market is multifaceted, with its impact varying significantly across different sectors. In manufacturing, AI-driven automation has introduced robots that can perform tasks ranging from assembling products to managing entire production lines with precision and efficiency. While this shift has led to job displacements, particularly for routine manual tasks, it has also created new positions in robot maintenance, programming, and system management, which demand new skills. Similarly, AI has transformed roles in the financial sector by taking over repetitive tasks such as data entry and analysis, allowing human employees to focus on more strategic activities such as client management and decision-making support. However, this transition requires current employees to adapt and acquire new capabilities to work alongside intelligent systems.

In the creative industries, AI's role is often viewed with skepticism, yet it has proven to be a collaborator rather than a usurper. AI tools in these fields assist in data-driven decision-making, enhance creativity through pattern recognition, and provide personalized content creation, which broadens the scope of creative jobs rather than replacing them. Meanwhile, the healthcare sector benefits from AI in diagnostics and patient care management, which can lead to job modifications rather than outright displacement. Here, AI empowers healthcare professionals by providing tools that offer deeper insights and diagnostics support, enhancing their ability to treat patients more effectively.

Economic Theories

Understanding AI's impact on the labor market also requires a grasp of relevant economic theories. One such theory is the concept of 'creative destruction,' coined by economist Joseph Schumpeter, which suggests that introducing new technologies can lead to the demise of older industries and jobs but simultaneously create new markets and employment opportunities. This theory is particularly relevant in AI, where innovation often disrupts existing business models and opens avenues for new jobs and industries. Another critical theory is the 'skill-biased technological change,' which posits that technological advancements, such as AI, tend to increase the demand for skilled labor while reducing the demand for unskilled or routine jobs. This theory highlights the need for upskilling and reskilling initiatives to prepare the workforce for the demands of a more technologically advanced job market.

Case Study - Tesla

To illustrate these dynamics, consider the automotive industry, which has seen significant transformations due to

AI and automation. Companies like Tesla have pioneered the integration of AI in manufacturing and vehicle operations, leading to shifts in labor demands. While some manual jobs have been displaced, new roles focused on software development, AI integration, and system management have emerged, reshaping the industry's workforce.

Background

Tesla, founded by Elon Musk in 2003, has been at the forefront of integrating advanced technologies into its manufacturing processes and vehicle operations. Tesla's commitment to innovation has led to significant advancements in electric vehicle (EV) technology, autonomous driving, and AI-driven manufacturing processes.

Problem

The automotive industry has traditionally been labor-intensive, with many manufacturing processes relying on human labor. Tesla aimed to revolutionize this by integrating AI and automation to improve efficiency, reduce costs, and enhance the quality of its vehicles. This integration, however, posed challenges related to shifts in labor demands and the need for a highly skilled workforce capable of managing advanced technologies.

Objective

Tesla's main objective was to pioneer AI's use in its manufacturing processes and vehicle operations, leading to a more efficient production system and advanced autonomous driving capabilities. This also included addressing the resultant shifts in labor demands and ensuring the workforce was equipped to handle new technological advancements.

Approach:

1. **AI in Manufacturing:**
   - **Gigafactories:** Tesla built highly automated Gigafactories that use AI and robotics to streamline the production of batteries and electric vehicles. These factories are designed to scale production rapidly while maintaining high efficiency and quality.
   - **Automation and Robotics:** Tesla integrated AI-driven robots and automated systems to

handle tasks such as welding, painting, assembly, and quality control. These robots are programmed to perform precise and repetitive tasks with minimal human intervention.

- **Predictive Maintenance:** AI algorithms monitor machinery and predict maintenance needs, reducing downtime and ensuring smooth operations.

2. **AI in Vehicle Operations:**
   - **Autopilot and Full Self-Driving (FSD):** Tesla's AI-powered Autopilot and FSD systems are designed to assist with driving tasks and eventually enable fully autonomous driving. These systems use neural networks to process data from cameras, sensors, and radar to make real-time driving decisions.

   - **Over-the-Air Updates:** Tesla vehicles receive over-the-air software updates that enhance the functionality of AI systems, improve performance, and add new features, ensuring that the cars remain cutting-edge without requiring physical modifications.

3. **Addressing Labor Shifts:**

- **Workforce Training:** Tesla invested in retraining programs to equip its workforce with the skills to manage and maintain AI and automated systems. This included training in robotics, AI programming, and advanced manufacturing techniques.

- **Job Creation in New Areas:** While automation reduced the need for certain manual labor positions, it created new opportunities in AI development, robotics maintenance, and software engineering. Tesla focused on balancing automation and human labor to optimize productivity and innovation.

Results:

1. **Increased Efficiency and Production:**

- Tesla's Gigafactories, powered by AI and automation, significantly increased production capacity and efficiency. The streamlined processes allowed Tesla to scale production to meet the growing demand for electric vehicles.

- The use of predictive maintenance reduced downtime and improved overall manufacturing efficiency.

2. **Enhanced Vehicle Capabilities:**

   - The AI-driven Autopilot and FSD systems provided Tesla vehicles with advanced autonomous driving capabilities, setting a benchmark in the automotive industry.

   - Regular over-the-air updates ensured Tesla owners benefited from continuous improvements and new features, enhancing the driving experience.

3. **Shift in Labor Demands:**

   - Integrating AI and automation led to a shift in labor demands, with a decreased need for manual labor and an increased demand for skilled workers in AI, robotics, and software engineering.

   - Tesla's investment in workforce training helped mitigate the impact of this shift, enabling employees to transition to new roles within the company.

4. **Industry Influence:**
   - Tesla's pioneering efforts in integrating AI into manufacturing and vehicle operations influenced the broader automotive industry. Competitors began adopting similar technologies to enhance their production processes and vehicle capabilities.
   - Tesla's success demonstrated the potential of AI to revolutionize manufacturing and operational efficiency, encouraging further innovation across various industries.

Conclusion

Tesla's integration of AI in manufacturing and vehicle operations represents a significant advancement in the automotive industry. By leveraging AI and automation, Tesla improved production efficiency, enhanced vehicle capabilities, and addressed shifts in labor demands through workforce training and job creation in new technological areas. This case study highlights the transformative impact of AI on traditional industries and underscores the importance of preparing the workforce for technological advancements. Tesla's pioneering efforts continue to set the standard for innovation and efficiency in the automotive sector.

Case Study - Amazon

Another retail sector example is Amazon's use of AI and robotics in its fulfillment centers. While automation has streamlined inventory management and delivery processes, it has also necessitated roles that oversee AI operations, including technicians and engineers who ensure the smooth functioning of these automated systems.

Background

Amazon, the global e-commerce giant, has revolutionized the retail industry by extensively using artificial intelligence (AI) and robotics in its fulfillment centers. These technologies have allowed Amazon to efficiently handle the immense volume of orders and maintain its promise of fast delivery, including the renowned Amazon Prime two-day shipping.

Problem

As Amazon's customer base grew exponentially, it faced challenges scaling its fulfillment operations to meet the increasing demand for fast and accurate order processing. Traditional manual processes were insufficient to efficiently handle the sheer volume of orders, leading to potential delays, errors, and increased labor costs.

Objective

The primary objective was integrating AI and robotics into Amazon's fulfillment centers to improve efficiency, accuracy, and speed in order processing while optimizing labor utilization.

Approach:

1. **Robotics Integration:**

   - **Kiva Systems Acquisition:** In 2012, Amazon acquired Kiva Systems, a robotics company, which was a pivotal move in integrating robotics into its fulfillment operations. Kiva robots are now a core component of Amazon's fulfillment centers.

   - **Robotic Fulfillment Systems:** Kiva robots are designed to transport shelves of products to human workers who pick items for orders. This system reduces workers' time walking around the warehouse and allows them to focus on selecting and packing.

2. **AI-Powered Automation:**

- **Inventory Management:** AI algorithms manage inventory placement within the warehouse to optimize space and ensure that high-demand items are easily accessible. This dynamic storage system adjusts real-time inventory locations based on demand patterns.

- **Order Fulfillment Optimization:** AI systems analyze order data to determine the most efficient way to pick, pack, and ship items. This includes optimizing packing processes to minimize shipping costs and delivery times.

- **Predictive Maintenance:** AI monitors the condition of robotic systems and other machinery to predict maintenance needs, preventing downtime and ensuring continuous operations.

3. **Enhanced Worker Efficiency:**
- **Human-Robot Collaboration:** Robots handle the transportation of items, while humans focus

on tasks that require more skill and decision-making, such as picking fragile items or packing orders. This collaboration enhances overall productivity.

- **Worker Safety and Ergonomics:** Robotic systems help decrease physical strain and the risk of injuries by reducing the amount of walking and heavy lifting required of human workers.

Results:

1. **Increased Efficiency and Speed:**

- Integrating Kiva robots and AI systems has significantly increased the speed and efficiency of Amazon's order fulfillment process. Robots can quickly transport items to workers, reducing order processing times.
- AI-driven inventory management and order fulfillment optimization have minimized delays and ensured faster delivery times, meeting customer expectations for rapid shipping.

2. **Enhanced Accuracy and Reduced Errors:**

- AI systems improve the accuracy of inventory tracking and order processing, reducing the likelihood of errors such as incorrect or missing items in shipments.
- The precise coordination between robots and human workers ensures that orders are fulfilled accurately and efficiently.

3. **Cost Savings and Labor Optimization:**

- Automation has led to substantial cost savings by reducing labor costs and improving operational efficiency. The need for a sizeable manual workforce has decreased, allowing Amazon to reallocate resources to other areas.
- Predictive maintenance has minimized downtime and maintenance costs, further enhancing operational efficiency.

4. **Scalability and Flexibility:**

- The scalable nature of AI and robotic systems allows Amazon to quickly expand its fulfillment capacity to accommodate peak shopping periods, such as holidays and sales events.

- The flexibility of these systems enables Amazon to adapt to changing demand patterns and efficiently manage its vast inventory.

Conclusion

Amazon's strategic integration of AI and robotics in its fulfillment centers has revolutionized its logistics operations, setting a new standard for the e-commerce industry. Using Kiva robots and AI-driven systems has significantly improved efficiency, accuracy, and speed of order processing while optimizing labor utilization and reducing costs. This case study demonstrates the transformative impact of AI and robotics on fulfillment operations. It highlights the importance of continuous innovation in maintaining competitive advantage in the fast-paced e-commerce sector.

Amazon's success with AI and robotics is a benchmark for other companies looking to enhance their logistics and fulfillment operations, showcasing the potential of advanced technologies to drive operational excellence and customer satisfaction.

Social Equity Concerns

As AI reshapes the employment landscape, addressing concerns regarding social equity and access to new opportunities is imperative. The risk of widening the inequality gap is real if proactive measures are not taken to ensure that the benefits of AI-driven job creation are broadly accessible. Initiatives aimed at providing equitable access to education and training in AI-related fields are crucial. These should be designed to reach diverse demographic groups, particularly those traditionally underrepresented in tech-related fields, ensuring that everyone has a fair chance to participate in and benefit from the AI-driven economy.

Visual Element: Infographic on AI's Impact Across Sectors

Below is an infographic to provide a clearer understanding of how AI impacts various industries. It highlights key sectors affected by AI, types of jobs impacted, new roles created, and essential skills for the future. This visual aid is designed to help you visualize the shifts occurring across different fields, aiding in a better understanding of where opportunities for growth and development lie.

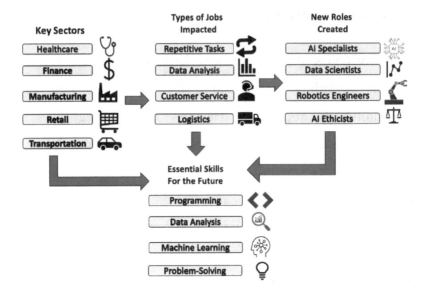

Figure 5 - AI Impacts to Industry

As we continue to explore the profound changes AI is bringing to the workplace, it becomes increasingly clear that the narrative is not solely about displacement but about transformation and opportunity. The ongoing challenge for developers, policymakers, and educators is to navigate this shift thoughtfully and inclusively, ensuring that AI's benefits are distributed equitably across society and fostering an environment where innovation leads to economic growth and societal advancement.

126

6.2 Ethical Considerations in AI and Automation

Worker Rights

As AI and automation technologies increasingly integrate into the workplace, the ethical implications for worker rights become a pressing concern. Automating tasks that humans traditionally perform raises fundamental questions about workers' security, dignity, and rights. One of the core ethical considerations is the risk of job displacement without adequate social safeguards, which can lead to significant economic and psychological distress for affected individuals. Protecting worker rights in this context means adhering to existing labor laws and evolving these laws to accommodate new realities. For instance, there needs to be a critical examination of fair labor practices when machines replace human roles. Are workers being fairly compensated for the increased productivity that automation brings?

Furthermore, issues such as surveillance and monitoring through AI technologies in the workplace must be carefully managed. While such practices can enhance efficiency, they should not infringe upon the privacy or autonomy of employees. Clear guidelines and regulations must be developed and enforced to ensure that monitoring does not overstep ethical boundaries, balancing organizational needs and personal privacy.

Reskilling and Upskilling

The ethical responsibilities of governments and corporations in the reskilling and upskilling workers displaced or affected by AI are immense. As specific jobs become obsolete, there is a moral imperative to ensure that the workforce is included. This involves substantial investment in education and training programs that can help workers transition to new roles that AI and automation are creating. For example, as AI transforms the retail industry, cashiers and inventory clerks facing job redundancy should have opportunities to retrain for more tech-focused roles, such as AI system monitors or data analysts within the same company. This not only helps individuals maintain employment but also aids companies in retaining valuable, experienced workers. Corporations, in partnership with educational institutions and governments, should actively develop programs that provide the necessary skills training tailored to the evolving job market. This commitment to workforce development reflects a broader ethical stance that values human capital for its economic output and as a fundamental aspect of societal well-being.

Transparency in Automation

Transparency in decisions related to workplace automation and AI integration is crucial for building trust and acceptance among workers. Employees are more likely to embrace change when they understand what is happening and how it affects them. Therefore, it is essential for companies to communicate clearly about the introduction of AI technologies, the reasons behind these decisions, the expected impacts, and the measures in place to support employees during transitions. For example, suppose a company decides to implement an AI system that automates specific tasks. In that case, it should provide a clear explanation to affected employees about why this change is necessary, how it will improve operations, and, most importantly, what the company is doing to mitigate any negative impacts on the workforce. This could include detailed information about reskilling opportunities, job role changes, and workplace practice enhancements. Transparency not only alleviates fears and builds confidence but also reinforces the ethical responsibility of businesses to treat their employees with respect and dignity.

Ethical Transition Frameworks

Developing frameworks for ethically transitioning workforces in the age of AI and automation is a complex challenge that requires a multifaceted approach. These frameworks should encompass a range of strategies from policy-making to organizational changes, all aimed at supporting employees through the transition. A key component is the ethical redeployment of workers, which involves identifying alternative employee roles within the organization as specific tasks become automated.

Another aspect is the creation of support systems that address the emotional and psychological impacts of job changes due to AI integration. Additionally, there needs to be a focus on creating inclusive policies that ensure all employees, regardless of their job function or background, have access to training and new opportunities. This might involve tailored training programs considering varying levels of education and technical proficiency, ensuring that no group is disproportionately disadvantaged by technological advancements. By adopting a holistic and inclusive approach to workforce transitions, organizations can ethically navigate the challenges of automation, fostering a work environment that is both productive and respectful of worker rights and dignity.

6.3 Preparing the Workforce for an AI-Driven Future

As AI continues redefining the work landscape, the imperative to adapt educational strategies and foster robust partnerships becomes increasingly evident. We must address the immediate skills gaps that arise as industries integrate more AI-driven technologies. Still, we also need to lay the groundwork for continuous learning to enable the workforce to thrive in a future where AI plays a central role. Educational initiatives play a pivotal role in this adaptation by equipping the current and future workforce with the necessary skills to navigate an AI-enhanced job market.

Initiatives such as specialized AI training programs in community colleges, vocational schools, and online platforms are crucial. These programs offer foundational knowledge in AI technologies and practical applications tailored to various sectors. For instance, a program might teach healthcare professionals how to interact with AI diagnostic tools or guide manufacturing workers in managing AI-driven production lines.

Beyond technical skills, these educational initiatives also emphasize critical thinking and problem-solving in an AI context, ensuring that workers can adapt to new challenges as AI technologies evolve. Moreover, integrating AI education in primary and secondary schools prepares the next generation from an early age, fostering an adaptable and fluent mindset in the languages of technology and innovation.

Public-private partnerships serve as a vital bridge between the theoretical knowledge provided in educational settings and the practical demands of the job market. These partnerships often involve collaborations between governments, academic institutions, technology companies, and industry leaders, aiming to create training programs that align with market needs. For example, a tech company might partner with a university to offer internships and co-op programs that provide students hands-on experience in AI projects. These partnerships enhance educational programs' relevance and facilitate smoother transitions for students from education to employment, ensuring that the workforce is ready to tackle the challenges and opportunities that AI brings.

Inclusive policymaking is another cornerstone of preparing the workforce for an AI-driven future. As AI technologies transform industries, the benefits and opportunities they create must be accessible to all segments of society. This requires policies that promote AI literacy and skills development across diverse demographic groups and address the barriers that might prevent these groups from accessing education and job opportunities in AI-related fields. Policies need to consider factors such as socioeconomic backgrounds, geographic locations, and existing educational disparities to create truly inclusive programs. This might involve providing scholarships, creating remote learning opportunities, or setting up community-based training centers in underserved areas.

Case Example: AI Education Initiative in Scandinavia

A notable example of a successful initiative that has significantly prepared a segment of the workforce for the AI era is the Scandinavian AI Education Program. Launched as a collaboration between multiple Scandinavian governments and private sector leaders in technology, the program focuses on integrating AI education across all levels of schooling, from primary to tertiary education. It also offers extensive retraining programs for existing workers across various sectors, from agriculture to finance, ensuring that the current workforce is not left behind as industries adopt more AI-driven processes.

The program's success is primarily due to its comprehensive approach, which includes curriculum development, teacher training, and partnerships with AI companies for internships and job placements. Additionally, the program strongly emphasizes inclusivity, providing tailored resources and support for underrepresented groups in the tech sector, such as women and rural populations. The results have been impressive, with significant increases in AI literacy levels across the population and a smoother transition for industries adopting AI technologies, marked by a boost in productivity and innovation.

6.4 Case Study: AI Automation Outages in Air Traffic Control

Scenario: Air traffic control (ATC) is fully automated using advanced AI systems that manage the flow of aircraft in the skies, ensuring safe distances between planes, optimizing flight paths, and handling communications between aircraft and ground control. This has led to a significant reduction in human ATC jobs, with AI systems taking over most of the critical functions. However, what happens if the AI automation system gets hacked or encounters a severe bug that brings the entire system down?

Potential Impacts:

1. **Immediate Consequences:**

   - **Safety Risks:** Without AI automation, the immediate risk is to the safety of aircraft in the air. Planes rely on constant communication and instructions from ATC to avoid collisions and manage landing sequences.

   - **Operational Disruptions:** The entire air traffic network could face severe disruptions, leading to delayed flights, grounded planes, and chaotic airport operations.

   - **Economic Impact:** The aviation industry could suffer significant financial losses due to canceled flights, refunds, and compensations.

2. **Backup Systems and Contingencies:**

- **Human Controllers:** Despite automation, a team of human air traffic controllers would still be necessary as a backup system. These controllers would need to be trained and ready to take over manually in case of system failure.

- **Redundant Systems:** Having redundant AI systems that can take over in case the primary system fails. These systems would need to be regularly tested and updated.

- **Manual Override:** Development of robust manual override systems that allow human operators to intervene and manage critical tasks.

- **Emergency Protocols:** Well-defined emergency protocols and drills to ensure a swift and efficient transition from automated to manual control.

Recovery and Contingency Planning:

1. **Immediate Response:**

- **Emergency Activation:** Human ATC operators would be immediately activated to manage the air traffic manually.

- **Communication:** Establish clear communication channels between human controllers, pilots, and airports to manage the transition smoothly.
- **Coordination:** Coordinated efforts with aviation authorities and airlines to prioritize flights and manage airport operations.

2. **Long-term Strategies:**

- **Resilience Training:** Continuous training programs for human ATC staff to keep their skills sharp and ensure they can handle emergency situations.
- **System Upgrades:** Regular upgrades and maintenance of AI systems to prevent bugs and enhance security measures against hacking.
- **Simulation Drills:** Conduct regular simulation drills involving both AI and human controllers to ensure readiness for any contingency.
- **Cross-training:** Cross-train staff to handle multiple roles within ATC operations to provide flexibility in emergencies.

Historical Precedents:

1. **FAA System Outage (2015):**

   - In August 2015, a significant technical failure in the FAA's En Route Automation Modernization (ERAM) system caused widespread delays and cancellations across the United States. The system, which manages high-altitude traffic, experienced a software glitch.

   - **Contingency Measures:** Air traffic controllers had to revert to manual processes, coordinating closely with airlines and airports to manage the disruption. The incident highlighted the need for robust backup systems and better contingency planning.

2. **British Airways IT Failure (2017):**

   - In May 2017, British Airways experienced a major IT system failure, leading to the cancellation of hundreds of flights and stranding thousands of passengers. The outage was caused by a power supply issue that affected the airline's data center.

- **Response:** British Airways had to manually manage passenger information, flight schedules, and communications. The incident underscored the importance of having redundant systems and manual backup procedures.

3. **CrowdStrike Cyberattack (2024):**

   - In February 2024, a cyberattack targeting CrowdStrike's AI-powered cybersecurity system led to a significant breach, affecting multiple critical infrastructures, including air traffic control systems globally. The attack resulted in days of flight backups and the cancellation of thousands of flights worldwide.

   - **Contingency Measures:** Air traffic controllers had to take manual control of flight operations, working around the clock to ensure safety and manage the backlog. The aviation industry collaborated with cybersecurity experts to contain the breach and restore automated systems. This incident highlighted the vulnerability of interconnected systems and the critical need for robust cybersecurity measures and human oversight.

4. **CrowdStrike Cyberattack (July 2024):**

- In July 2024, another cyberattack targeted CrowdStrike's systems, causing significant disruptions in air traffic control. This attack once again resulted in thousands of flights being canceled and widespread delays, affecting air travel globally.

- **Response and Recovery:** The incident forced the aviation industry to reevaluate its dependency on AI automation and highlighted the importance of having robust backup systems. Human controllers were once again essential in managing the crisis, underscoring the need for continuous training and preparedness for such scenarios. This second major incident in a year emphasized the necessity of implementing stronger cybersecurity protocols and developing more resilient AI systems.

Conclusion:

The case of fully automated air traffic control illustrates the critical need for robust contingency planning and the importance of maintaining human oversight even in highly automated systems. While AI automation can significantly enhance efficiency and safety in the aviation industry, the potential risks associated with system failures or cyber-attacks must be meticulously managed. Ensuring that human controllers are trained and ready to step in, developing redundant systems, and conducting regular drills are essential components of a resilient air traffic management system. Historical incidents like the FAA system outage, British Airways IT failure, and the recent CrowdStrike cyberattack provide valuable lessons in managing and mitigating the impacts of automation failures.

As this chapter closes, we are reminded of the transformative potential of AI and the importance of proactive preparation in harnessing this potential responsibly. Educational initiatives, public-private partnerships, and inclusive policies are not just reactive measures to changes brought about by AI but proactive steps towards a future where technology and humanity progress hand in hand. Looking ahead, the next chapter will delve into cultural sensitivity in AI development, exploring how we can ensure that AI technologies respect and reflect the diverse values and needs of global communities, thereby enriching the tapestry of AI's impact on society.

Chapter 7: Cultural Sensitivity in AI Development

Imagine strolling through a vast, vibrant market that spans the globe—each stall bursting with its colors, flavors, and sounds. Now, picture creating a technology meant to serve each vendor and customer in this market with respect and understanding of their unique cultural backgrounds. This challenge lies at the heart of integrating cultural sensitivity into AI development. As you venture into creating AI solutions for a global stage, recognizing and embracing cultural diversity becomes beneficial and imperative. This chapter delves deep into the nuances of cultural context in AI ethics, offering you a compass to navigate this complex terrain and ensuring your AI solutions are as culturally nuanced as they are technologically advanced.

7.1 The Role of Cultural Context in AI Ethics

Cultural Variability in Ethical Norms

The spectrum of ethical norms across different cultures is as broad and varied as the languages spoken across the globe. Each culture brings values, practices, and expectations that deeply influence perceptions of what is considered ethical. For instance, the concept of privacy varies significantly between Western cultures, which may emphasize individual rights, and Eastern cultures, where communal values prevail. This variability can profoundly affect how AI technologies are received and can determine their success or failure in different markets. As you develop AI solutions, understanding these nuances is crucial. It requires a commitment to recognize, deeply understand, and respect these differences, integrating them into the fabric of AI development processes.

Integrating Local Ethics in Global AI Solutions

Integrating local ethical considerations into AI solutions developed for the global market is akin to a chef creating a dish that needs to appeal to palates from multiple continents. It requires both sensitivity and a nuanced understanding of local tastes. For AI developers, this means engaging with local stakeholders during the development process to gain insights into the cultural context and ethical expectations. One effective strategy is the establishment of advisory panels composed of local experts and representatives who can provide ongoing guidance and feedback. Additionally, employing culturally diverse development teams can enhance the ability to imbue AI systems with a broader spectrum of ethical perspectives, making these systems more adaptable and acceptable across different cultural settings.

Case Studies of Cultural Missteps

The path of integrating cultural sensitivity into AI is strewn with lessons from past missteps. One notable example involves a voice recognition system developed by a leading tech company that failed to recognize accents from several non-Western countries. This oversight led to significant user frustration and market withdrawal, highlighting the consequences of overlooking cultural diversity in AI functionalities. Another example is an AI-driven advertising system that inadvertently perpetuated gender stereotypes, offending users across various demographics and leading to a public relations crisis. These cases underline the critical importance of cultural sensitivity in AI development and the potential repercussions of its neglect.

Guidelines for Culturally Sensitive AI Development

To avoid such pitfalls and to foster AI systems that are truly global in their appeal and functionality, here are some actionable guidelines:

- **Conduct Comprehensive Cultural Audits**: Before deployment, AI systems should undergo rigorous reviews to ensure they align with local cultural norms and ethical standards. This involves testing the systems across different cultural settings and making necessary adjustments.

- **Implement Continuous Learning and Adaptation Mechanisms**: AI systems should be designed to learn from cultural interactions and evolve accordingly. This adaptability allows AI systems to stay relevant and sensitive to cultural shifts and nuances over time.

- **Foster Open Dialogue**: Maintain an ongoing conversation about cultural sensitivity within AI development teams and with external stakeholders. This open dialogue fosters a deeper understanding and awareness of cultural issues.

- **Develop Inclusive Policies and Practices**: Establish policies that explicitly address the need for cultural diversity and inclusivity within AI development processes. This includes diversity in hiring, training programs on cultural competence, and inclusive design practices.

Visual Element: Cultural Sensitivity Checklist

Below is a detailed checklist to aid in the practical application of these guidelines. This tool is designed to help you ensure that every phase of AI development, from design to deployment, considers and respects cultural diversity, enhancing the global applicability and acceptance of AI technologies.

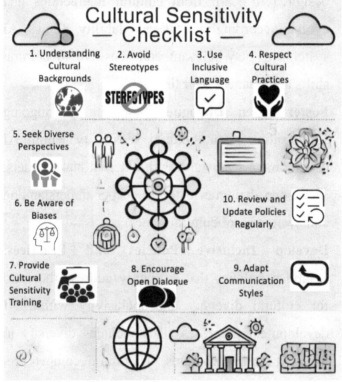

Figure 6 - Cultural Sensitivity Checklist

Cultural Sensitivity Checklist:

1. **Understand Cultural Backgrounds:**

   o **Icon:** Globe with people

   o **Description:** Gain knowledge about different cultural backgrounds and histories.

2. **Avoid Stereotypes:**

   o **Icon:** No symbol "Stereotypes"

   o **Description:** Refrain from making generalized assumptions about people based on their culture.

3. **Use Inclusive Language:**

   o **Icon:** Speech bubble with a checkmark

   o **Description:** Ensure that your language is inclusive and respectful of all cultures.

4. **Respect Cultural Practices:**

   o **Icon:** Hands holding a heart

   o **Description:** Show respect for cultural practices and traditions.

5. **Seek Diverse Perspectives:**

   o **Icon:** Magnifying glass over people

   o **Description:** Actively seek and consider perspectives from diverse cultural backgrounds.

6. **Be Aware of Biases:**

   o **Icon:** Brain with a bias symbol

o **Description:** Recognize and address any personal or systemic biases.

7. **Provide Cultural Sensitivity Training:**
   o **Icon:** Training or workshop symbol
   o **Description:** Offer training programs to educate about cultural sensitivity.

8. **Encourage Open Dialogue:**
   o **Icon:** Two speech bubbles
   o **Description:** Foster an environment where open and respectful dialogue about cultural differences is encouraged.

9. **Adapt Communication Styles:**
   o **Icon:** Adjusting arrows with a speech bubble
   o **Description:** Modify communication styles to be appropriate for different cultural contexts.

10. **Review and Update Policies Regularly:**
    o **Icon:** Checklist with a refresh symbol
    o **Description:** Continuously review and update policies to ensure they reflect cultural sensitivity.

Navigating the cultural dimensions of AI ethics involves more than just avoiding missteps; it encompasses a proactive embrace of diversity that enriches AI solutions, making them more thoughtful, inclusive, and effective globally. As you continue to explore and integrate these cultural considerations into your AI projects, remember that each step taken towards cultural sensitivity broadens the reach of your technologies and deepens their impact, fostering a world where AI operates across cultural boundaries and respects and celebrates them.

7.2 Case Studies: AI Ethics Across Cultures

The development and deployment of AI technologies in various Asian contexts unveil a tapestry of ethical considerations deeply rooted in cultural values and social norms unique to each region. In China, for instance, the Confucian philosophy emphasizing harmony and collective welfare influences how AI technologies are developed and utilized. AI applications in public surveillance and social scoring systems reflect these values, prioritizing societal stability and harmony but raising concerns about individual privacy and autonomy from a Western perspective. In contrast, Japan, which blends its Shinto traditions with a strong drive for technological innovation, focuses on how AI can enhance societal well-being while respecting the 'Kami' or spirits inherent in all objects, including technological devices. This cultural backdrop influences the ethical frameworks within which AI systems are designed, prompting developers to create efficient and harmonious technologies with traditional beliefs and practices.

The discourse between Western and Eastern ethical perspectives on AI offers a fascinating exploration of divergence and convergence. Western approaches often emphasize individual rights and freedoms, strongly focusing on privacy, autonomy, and informed consent. This is evident in regulatory environments such as Europe's GDPR, which prioritizes individual control over personal data. Eastern perspectives, however, often prioritize the collective good and societal harmony over individual rights.

In South Korea, for example, AI technologies in urban planning and public safety reflect a group-oriented ethos, focusing on societal benefits such as reduced traffic accidents and crime rates. However, areas of convergence are also evident, particularly in the realm of AI ethics concerning human dignity and the avoidance of harm. Western and Eastern cultures show a growing consensus on the need for AI technologies to be developed to prevent damage and discrimination, underscoring a universal ethical concern that transcends cultural boundaries.

Indigenous perspectives on AI, often overlooked in mainstream AI ethics dialogues, bring unique viewpoints that enrich our understanding of ethical AI development. Indigenous communities worldwide hold deep connections with their environments and a holistic view of existence, emphasizing the interdependence of all life forms. This worldview can offer profound insights into how AI might be developed with a greater focus on sustainability and ecological balance. For instance, AI applications used in environmental monitoring can benefit from indigenous knowledge systems emphasizing long-term ecological cycles and sustainable resource management. Including Indigenous perspectives in AI ethics broadens the discourse and ensures that AI development aligns with diverse value systems. This promotes a more inclusive approach to technology that respects all life forms and their interconnections.

The success stories of cross-cultural AI projects highlight effective strategies for integrating diverse cultural perspectives and achieving significant outcomes. One such project involved a multinational team that designed a health monitoring AI system used across several African and Asian countries. The project's success hinged on its inclusive approach to design, which involved local healthcare professionals and patients in the design process, ensuring the system was adapted to meet diverse healthcare practices and patient needs. The AI system was equipped to handle multiple languages and incorporated locally relevant health indicators, significantly improving patient outcomes and healthcare efficiency in these regions. Another successful project was the development of a multilingual AI-driven educational platform that adapted its content to the cultural contexts of different areas, enhancing students' engagement and learning outcomes. These projects demonstrate that when AI development actively incorporates diverse cultural insights, the technology not only gains wider acceptance but also becomes more impactful, addressing different communities' specific needs and values worldwide.

Navigating the complexities of cultural diversity in AI ethics requires a nuanced understanding of how cultural contexts influence ethical perceptions and the practical applications of AI. By examining the varied approaches and integrating diverse perspectives, AI development can advance in a manner that is not only technologically sound but also ethically robust and culturally sensitive. This approach ensures that AI technologies are accepted across different societies and enriches these societies by respecting and upholding their unique cultural values and ethical standards.

7.3 Designing AI for Global Diversity

In the endeavor to craft AI systems that resonate globally, the principles of inclusive design stand as beacons guiding the way. These principles are not just about avoiding exclusion but proactively ensuring that AI systems are accessible, understandable, and usable across a vast spectrum of global diversity, encompassing cultural, linguistic, and socio-economic dimensions. To start, inclusivity in AI necessitates a design philosophy that embeds diversity at every stage of the development process—from conceptualization to deployment. This involves rigorous user research to understand the varied contexts in which the AI will operate, ensuring the system can adapt to and respect a range of cultural norms and languages. Moreover, socio-economic inclusivity means designing AI systems accessible to users with varying income levels, education, and technological access. This could involve developing simplified interfaces for users with limited tech literacy or ensuring the AI application functions effectively on lower-end hardware commonly used in less affluent regions.

The development of such universally adaptive AI systems is supported by various tools and frameworks designed to aid developers in embracing global diversity. For instance, cross-cultural design toolkits provide guidelines and best practices for creating interfaces that accommodate cultural differences in color meaning, layout preferences, and interaction styles. Language localization tools go beyond simple translation to adapt AI interactions to different languages' idiomatic and cultural nuances, enhancing user comprehension and engagement. Additionally, frameworks like the Inclusive Design Principles focus on broader aspects of accessibility and usability, advocating for flexible user configurations that can adapt to various physical, cognitive, and environmental constraints. Employing these tools broadens the reach of AI systems and deepens their impact by making them more relevant and user-friendly across diverse global contexts.

However, the path to creating globally diverse AI systems is challenging. One of the primary hurdles is the complexity of accurately understanding and integrating the myriad cultural nuances that influence user behavior and expectations. This task is compounded by the rapid pace of cultural change and the dynamic nature of global interactions, where yesterday's understanding may not fit today's reality. Another significant challenge is the technical difficulty of developing AI algorithms that can effectively adapt to a wide range of user inputs and environmental contexts. This often requires advanced AI capabilities like natural language understanding and contextual adaptation, which can be resource-intensive to develop and maintain.

To illustrate the practical application of these principles and tools, consider the case study of a globally inclusive AI-driven healthcare application designed to provide personalized health advice to users worldwide. Based in multiple countries, the development team employed a user-centered design approach, conducting extensive research to understand health management behaviors across different cultural contexts. They used localization tools to ensure the app was usable in multiple languages, including those with non-Latin scripts like Arabic and Mandarin, and adapted the content to reflect local dietary habits, health norms, and medical practices. The application also featured adjustable interface elements to accommodate varying levels of technological proficiency and accessibility needs. Despite challenges such as managing the vast amount of localized content and ensuring accurate cultural adaptation, the application successfully provided tailored, contextually appropriate health advice to a diverse user base, significantly improving health outcomes and user satisfaction in multiple regions.

This journey through the landscape of designing AI for global diversity highlights the necessity and benefits of creating inclusive AI systems that respect and adapt to the rich tapestry of international cultures, languages, and socio-economic conditions. As developers, by committing to these principles and leveraging available tools, you contribute to the technological advancement of AI and a more inclusive and equitable global society. The insights gained from this endeavor underscore the importance of diversity and inclusivity in driving the successful worldwide adoption and beneficial impact of AI technologies. As we move forward, let these principles light our path, guiding us to create AI solutions that are not only innovative but also profoundly respectful and inclusive of the diverse world we share.

Chapter 8: AI Ethics in a Globalized World

Imagine navigating the bustling corridors of the United Nations, where diplomats from diverse backgrounds converge to forge agreements that transcend borders and cultures. Now imagine a similar scenario in artificial intelligence (AI), where global leaders and ethicists gather to sculpt standards that ensure AI technologies benefit humanity while respecting the rich tapestry of global cultures. In this chapter, we delve into the intricate world of global ethical standards for AI, exploring existing frameworks, the challenges of harmonization, the pivotal roles international organizations play, and the spirited debates surrounding universal ethical standards for AI.

8.1 Global Ethical Standards for AI: Possibilities and Challenges

Existing Global Standards for AI Ethics

As you, the AI developer, architect, or ethicist, strive to embed ethical considerations into your work, you are not navigating uncharted waters. Several frameworks and guidelines have been established to guide ethical AI development. For instance, the OECD Principles on AI, adopted by over 40 countries, outline values such as inclusivity, transparency, and accountability, aiming to foster trust and promote the responsible deployment of AI technologies. Similarly, the IEEE Global Initiative on Ethics of Autonomous and Intelligent Systems offers detailed recommendations focused on prioritizing human well-being in the age of AI. These standards are foundational blocks that guide you in integrating ethical considerations into your AI solutions.

However, the applicability and scope of these guidelines can vary significantly. While some offer broad principles, others delve into granular specifics, which can be both a boon and a bane. For you, the challenge lies in deciphering which standards are most relevant and how they can be effectively applied in your specific context. This requires a deep understanding of the guidelines and an ability to adapt them to fit the cultural and regulatory landscapes in which your AI systems will operate.

Harmonizing Diverse Ethical Standards

The quest to harmonize these diverse ethical standards into a cohesive global framework is akin to conducting an orchestra where each instrument brings a distinct sound.

The harmonization process involves aligning varied ethical perspectives from different cultural, social, and political contexts, which is no small feat. The challenge here is to find common ground while respecting the uniqueness of each perspective, ensuring that the resulting standards are universally applicable and locally adaptable.

This endeavor is not just necessary; it's urgent. As AI technologies increasingly cross borders through international commerce and digital connectivity, a fragmented approach to AI ethics could lead to inconsistencies that hinder AI technologies' potential to address global challenges. The possibilities for harmonization include creating flexible frameworks that set out core principles while allowing for regional adaptations. These frameworks would need to be dynamic, evolving with technological advancements and shifts in societal values, much like amendments to a living constitution.

Role of International Organizations in AI Ethics

International organizations like the United Nations, the European Union, and the World Health Organization play a crucial role in this orchestration. These bodies have the convening power to bring together diverse stakeholders from around the globe, facilitating dialogues that bridge differences and foster consensus. For instance, the UN's activities around AI have included convening expert groups that draft recommendations reflecting a broad consensus among member states. Similarly, the EU has been instrumental in setting benchmarks for AI regulations that many consider gold standards, influencing policies beyond its borders.

These organizations also play a critical role in advocacy, education, and capacity building, helping member states and organizations understand the implications of AI ethics and integrate these principles into their national policies and corporate practices. For you, as someone involved in AI development, these organizations can provide valuable resources and a platform for engaging with global standards, ensuring your work aligns with international best practices.

Debating Universal Ethics for AI

Yet, the debate over whether universal ethical standards for AI are feasible or even desirable remains heated. Detractors argue that ethical absolutism in AI overlooks the profound cultural differences that shape moral judgments. They caution against a one-size-fits-all approach, which might impose alien or objectionable values on some cultures, potentially leading to conflicts and resistance. Proponents, however, argue that in a globally connected world, standard ethical guidelines are essential to ensure that AI technologies are developed and deployed in beneficial and fair ways to all humanity, regardless of geographical location.

This debate requires a delicate balance, recognizing the universal rights and values that must be upheld while allowing for cultural variations that do not infringe on these rights. Such discussions are vital as they shape the policies and practices that will guide the development of AI technologies in the future. As you engage with this debate, whether in forums, research, or practice, your insights and actions contribute to shaping a landscape where AI can indeed be a force for good, guided by ethical standards that respect universal human rights and cultural diversity.

Visual Element: Interactive Ethical AI Framework Exploration Tool

Below is an interactive tool to assist you in navigating these complex issues. This tool allows you to explore various global ethical AI frameworks, compare their principles, and understand their applications in different cultural contexts. By interacting with this tool, you can gain deeper insights into how global standards can be adapted to fit specific needs, enriching your understanding and application of AI ethics in a globalized world.

An example of an Interactive Ethical AI Framework Exploration Tool is the AI Fairness 360 (AIF360) toolkit developed by IBM. This toolkit provides a comprehensive set of metrics to test for biases in datasets and machine learning models. It also offers algorithms to mitigate these biases and an interactive web application to explore and visualize the results.

Key Features of AI Fairness 360:

1. **Bias Detection Metrics:**
   - AIF360 includes a variety of metrics to evaluate biases in training data and models. These metrics can measure disparate impact, equal opportunity, and statistical parity.

2. **Bias Mitigation Algorithms:**
   - The toolkit provides several algorithms to reduce bias, such as reweighing data

samples, adjusting model training processes, and modifying predictions to achieve fair outcomes.

3. **Interactive Web Application:**

- Users can interact with the AIF360 web application to visualize bias metrics and mitigation results. The interface allows for exploring different scenarios and the impact of various mitigation strategies on fairness.

4. **Comprehensive Documentation and Tutorials:**

- AIF360 includes detailed documentation and tutorials that guide users through assessing and mitigating bias in AI systems. These resources help practitioners understand and apply ethical AI principles effectively.

5. **Open Source and Extensible:**

- The open-source toolkit allows users to customize and extend its functionalities, ensuring that it can be tailored to specific needs and integrated into different AI development workflows.

Use Case Example:

Imagine a healthcare organization using AI to predict patient outcomes. By integrating AIF360 into their development process, they can:

1. **Assess Data Bias:**
   - They can use AIF360 metrics to detect biases in their patient data, such as disparities in predictions based on race or gender.

2. **Mitigate Bias:**
   - Apply bias mitigation algorithms provided by AIF360 to ensure that the AI model does not unfairly disadvantage any group.

3. **Visualize and Explore:**
   - Utilize the interactive web application to visualize the impact of different bias mitigation strategies and explore how changes improve fairness.

4. **Continuous Monitoring:**
   - Implement continuous monitoring using AIF360 to ensure that their AI system remains fair and unbiased as new data is introduced.

As we continue exploring the complexities of AI ethics in a globalized world, remember that each step you take to understand and apply these principles contributes to a broader effort. An effort to ensure AI technologies are innovative and influential and wielded with responsibility and deep respect for the diverse tapestry of human values and cultures.

8.2 Cross-Border AI Initiatives: Collaborating on Ethical Practices

In the realm of technology, particularly within the sphere of artificial intelligence, cross-border collaborations can unlock unprecedented innovations by merging diverse intellectual landscapes, resources, and perspectives. These initiatives often span continents, bringing together experts from vastly different cultural, legal, and ethical backgrounds to forge solutions that are not only technologically advanced but also culturally nuanced and ethically sound. However, integrating varied ethical considerations into these projects takes time and effort. It requires a delicate balance of respect, understanding, and adaptability among the participating entities.

One illustrative example of successful cross-border AI collaboration is the Global AI Health Alliance, a consortium of healthcare providers, AI technology firms, and academic institutions from North America, Europe, and Asia. This initiative focuses on developing AI-driven diagnostic tools that can be adapted to different health systems worldwide, respecting local medical practices and patient privacy laws. By pooling datasets from diverse populations and leveraging a wide range of expertise, the alliance has enhanced the accuracy and applicability of AI diagnostics across different regions, significantly improving patient outcomes while adhering to strict ethical standards tailored to each country's regulations.

Despite these successes, cross-border AI collaborations often need to overcome significant hurdles. Legal challenges are particularly daunting, as each country has its own set of regulations governing data privacy, intellectual property, and AI deployment, which can vary widely. Navigating this legal patchwork requires robust legal expertise and flexible project frameworks that can adapt to multiple legal systems. Ethical barriers also present substantial challenges, especially when collaborators have differing views on issues like data usage, bias mitigation, and the extent of automation acceptable in various applications. Moreover, cultural differences can lead to miscommunications and misunderstandings, potentially derailing projects or making implementations insensitive to local norms and practices.

Several best practices have been identified to overcome these challenges and foster ethical collaboration in cross-border AI projects. Open and continuous communication is crucial. Regular, clear, and transparent discussions among all stakeholders help align goals, set expectations, and resolve misunderstandings promptly. Utilizing collaborative tools that support real-time interaction and documentation can facilitate this process. Inclusivity is another critical practice; ensuring that all voices, especially those from underrepresented or marginalized groups, are heard and considered can lead to more ethically robust and universally acceptable AI solutions. Mutual respect and a commitment to understanding different cultural and ethical perspectives are fundamental to this process. Workshops and joint training sessions on ethical AI development can be instrumental in building a shared understanding and appreciation of diverse viewpoints.

Looking to the future, cross-border AI initiatives are poised to become increasingly prevalent as the global demand for sophisticated AI solutions continues to rise. Emerging technologies such as quantum computing and blockchain could play significant roles in these projects, offering new ways to securely manage data and enhance computational capabilities. Moreover, as international awareness of AI's ethical implications grows, we might see more structured global frameworks emerging to guide these collaborations effectively. These frameworks could streamline legal and ethical compliance, making it easier for international teams to work together towards common goals.

As you engage in or support cross-border AI projects, these insights into the challenges and best practices of ethical collaboration could be invaluable. Whether you are navigating complex legal landscapes or aligning diverse ethical standards, the goal remains to develop AI technologies that are not only innovative but also respectful of the global tapestry of cultures and values they aim to serve.

8.3 Global Governance of AI Ethics

The rapid proliferation of AI technologies across borders necessitates a robust global governance structure to oversee ethical development and deployment. This need stems from a universal concern: as AI systems influence everything from global finance to personal healthcare, the decisions they make can have profound implications. Without a coherent global governance framework, there is a risk that these technologies could exacerbate inequalities, infringe on privacy rights, or be used in ways that could cause harm, intentionally or unintentionally. Global governance in this context aims to establish standards and practices that ensure AI technologies are developed and used in ways that are beneficial and fair to all of humanity, regardless of geographical, cultural, or economic differences.

Various proposals have surfaced regarding how such governance structures might be designed. One suggestion involves the creation of an international AI regulatory body similar to the International Atomic Energy Agency (IAEA), which has a mandate to promote the safe, secure, and peaceful use of nuclear technologies. An analogous AI body could oversee the safe and ethical development of AI technologies, ensuring they comply with internationally agreed-upon standards. This body could facilitate cooperation between nations, help disseminate best practices, and provide a platform for addressing transnational AI-related issues. However, the establishment of such a governance body is challenging. Questions about jurisdiction, enforceability of regulations, and the balance of power between different nations need careful consideration. The effectiveness of such a body heavily depends on its ability to be truly representative and fair in considering the diverse interests and values of all global stakeholders.

A compelling case study in international AI regulation efforts is the European Union's approach to AI governance. The EU has been at the forefront of regulating AI, with comprehensive policies that address everything from data protection to ethical guidelines for AI development. One of the landmark regulations is the General Data Protection Regulation (GDPR), which, while primarily focused on data protection, has significant implications for AI by setting strict guidelines on data consent, a crucial aspect of AI development. The GDPR affects companies operating within the EU and has a global impact, as international companies must comply with these regulations to operate in the European market. Drafting, implementing, and enforcing these regulations involved extensive consultations with various stakeholders, rigorous debates, and adjustments to address concerns from industry players and consumer rights groups. The ongoing evolution of these regulations in response to emerging AI technologies and challenges provides a dynamic model of how robust and adaptive global AI governance might be achieved.

Several strategies can be considered for effective global AI governance that respects cultural diversity and promotes the ethical use of AI technologies:

1. Fostering transparency in AI development processes and decision-making is crucial. This means governments and organizations involved in AI development should openly share their methodologies, data sources, and impact assessments. Transparency builds trust and facilitates international scrutiny and collaboration, ensuring AI systems are held to the highest ethical standards.

2. Fostering inclusive dialogue and collaboration among various stakeholders is essential. This includes AI developers, policymakers, and representatives from marginalized communities who may be disproportionately affected by AI technologies. By involving diverse voices in the governance process, policies are more likely to be equitable and considerate of varied cultural norms and values.

3. A continuous effort should be made to build and update international legal frameworks that can adapt to the rapid advancements in AI technology.

These frameworks should be crafted to facilitate cooperation in AI research and development while ensuring that all nations have a say in shaping global standards.

Exploring global governance of AI ethics underscores the importance of coordinated international efforts in ensuring AI technologies serve the common good. As we reflect on the various facets of AI governance, from the need for robust structures to the challenges and strategies of implementing such frameworks, it becomes clear that our collective actions today will shape the ethical landscape of AI for future generations. This discussion sets the stage for the next chapter, which will delve into the ethical considerations of AI in specific applications, providing insights into applying these global principles in practical scenarios. As we move forward, let these discussions guide responsible and thoughtful engagement with AI technologies, ensuring they enhance our global society rather than diminish it.

Chapter 9: Addressing Global Challenges with Ethical AI

Imagine standing at the precipice of a world where the once clear and abundant rivers are running dry, forests - the earth's ancient sentinels - are diminishing, and the air carries whispers of vanished species. Now, visualize harnessing AI not as a mere tool of industrialization but as a steward of this planet's future, turning the tide against environmental degradation. In this chapter, we explore the profound role AI can play in environmental sustainability, weaving through the realms of climate change mitigation, ethical considerations, impactful case studies, and the visionary future of AI in this critical field. As you, a pivotal player in AI development, traverse through these insights, consider the technological possibilities and the ethical imperatives that should guide your endeavors.

9.1 AI for Environmental Sustainability

AI in Climate Change Mitigation

AI emerges as a powerful ally in the fight against climate change. Through predictive modeling, AI technologies can accurately forecast environmental changes, enabling proactive approaches to climate management. For instance,

AI models that predict weather patterns can be utilized to optimize agricultural practices, ensuring crops get planted at optimal times and reducing resource waste. Moreover, AI-driven resource optimization extends to energy management. AI-powered intelligent grids optimize electricity distribution based on real-time data, drastically reducing energy waste and enhancing the use of renewable energy sources.

Yet, AI's potential in climate change mitigation transcends predictive analytics and resource optimization. It also plays a critical role in carbon capture technologies, where AI algorithms enhance the efficiency of extracting carbon dioxide from the atmosphere, a crucial step towards reducing greenhouse gas levels. These AI solutions not only demonstrate the integration of advanced technology in combating climate change but also underscore the necessity of your role in steering these innovations toward maximum efficacy and minimal environmental impact.

Ethical Considerations in AI for Sustainability

Navigating the ethical landscape is paramount as you integrate AI into sustainability efforts. The deployment of AI in environmental projects must carefully consider data privacy, especially when monitoring involves collecting data from numerous sensors across various locations, potentially intruding into private spaces. Ensuring that data collection complies with stringent privacy standards and is transparent to the public is crucial for maintaining trust and ethical integrity.

Furthermore, the ecological impact of AI technologies must be considered. AI systems consume significant amounts of energy, particularly those requiring substantial computational power. Developing AI solutions that are not only effective but also energy-efficient is a critical challenge. Additionally, the lifecycle of AI hardware often involves environmentally detrimental mining practices for rare minerals and contributes to electronic waste. Addressing these issues involves designing sustainable AI systems in their application and throughout their entire lifecycle, from development to disposal.

Case Studies of AI in Environmental Projects

To ground these concepts in reality, let's examine some case studies where AI has been successfully integrated into environmental sustainability projects. One notable example involves a project in the Amazon rainforest, where AI-driven drones monitor deforestation activities, providing real-time data that enables swift action against illegal logging. Another case is an ocean cleanup project that uses AI to analyze satellite images and predict the accumulation points of plastic debris in the ocean, directing cleanup efforts more efficiently and effectively.

These examples illustrate AI's practical applications in environmental projects and highlight the ethical practices that guide these initiatives. By maintaining transparency in data usage, ensuring minimal impact on local ecosystems, and focusing on long-term sustainability, these projects set benchmarks for how AI can be ethically and effectively employed in environmental preservation.

Future Potential of AI in Sustainability

Looking ahead, AI's potential to advance environmental sustainability is boundless. Innovations such as AI-assisted genetic engineering could lead to the development of crops that require less water and are more resilient to ever-changing climate conditions, significantly reducing agriculture's environmental footprint. Additionally, AI could be pivotal in sustainable urban development, from optimizing traffic flows to reduce emissions to integrating renewable energy systems into intelligent urban infrastructures.

As you, an AI professional, forge ahead in your career, engaging with these technologies could shape the future of AI and this planet. Integrating AI into environmental sustainability is not just a technological journey but a moral imperative, urging you to wield this powerful tool with responsibility and foresight, ensuring a thriving planet for future generations.

9.2 Ethical AI in Healthcare: Global Case Studies

In healthcare, the integration of artificial intelligence (AI) unfolds a new chapter of innovation intertwined with profound ethical considerations. As you, a developer or healthcare professional, engage with AI technologies, the responsibility extends beyond technical implementation to encompass the ethical realms of equity, consent, and transparency. These principles are not merely idealistic goals but foundational elements that ensure AI tools in healthcare heal and uphold the dignity and rights of every patient they serve.

The deployment of AI within global health initiatives often aims to bridge the gap between advanced healthcare systems and underserved communities. AI's ability to analyze vast datasets can lead to breakthroughs in understanding diseases, optimizing treatment pathways, and predicting health outcomes with impressive accuracy. However, these advancements must be carefully balanced with considerations of equity. It is crucial to ensure that AI systems do not inadvertently widen health disparities by favoring data from more affluent populations, which tend to be overrepresented in medical research databases.

To address this, ethical AI deployment in healthcare involves rigorous protocols to ensure data diversity and algorithmic fairness. Additionally, obtaining informed consent becomes particularly challenging in AI-driven healthcare. The complexity of AI systems can make it difficult for patients to understand what they consent to, especially concerning how their data will be used. Therefore, transparent communication and consent processes become paramount, ensuring that patients retain control over their health information.

Balancing the rapid pace of innovation in AI with the ethical obligations to protect and respect patients and communities is a delicate task. Healthcare professionals and AI developers must work collaboratively to ensure that AI tools are designed and deployed in a manner that respects patient autonomy and promotes well-being. This involves continuous ethical training for AI teams and healthcare staff, ensuring they can identify and address potential ethical issues as they arise. Regular ethical reviews and updates to AI systems are also essential, ensuring they adapt to new health challenges and ethical standards.

Success stories from implementing ethical AI in healthcare offer valuable insights into effective practices. One example is a telemedicine project in rural Asia, where AI-powered diagnostic tools have been used to extend healthcare services to remote areas. The project faced initial challenges in gaining the trust of local communities unfamiliar with AI technology. By implementing community-engagement programs that explained the benefits and safety of the technology, alongside robust data protection measures, the project not only improved healthcare delivery but also ensured community members felt respected and involved in the healthcare process. Another example is an AI system used in Europe to predict patient deterioration. The system's developers strongly emphasized transparency, providing patients and healthcare providers with clear information on how the AI makes its predictions. This openness helped to build trust and facilitated the system's acceptance in a clinical setting.

However, the integration of AI into healthcare is challenging. One of the recurring issues is the risk of bias in AI algorithms, which can lead to disparities in healthcare outcomes. For instance, an AI system designed to assess patient risks for various surgeries might perform well on populations it was primarily trained on but less so on underrepresented populations. Addressing these biases requires continuous monitoring and recalibration of AI systems, alongside the inclusion of diverse datasets during the training phase. Another significant challenge is ensuring the security of patient data, particularly as cyber threats become more sophisticated. Developing robust cybersecurity measures and constant vigilance is crucial to protect sensitive health information.

The lessons learned from these challenges underscore the importance of a proactive approach to ethical considerations in AI-driven healthcare. Each step in developing and deploying AI technologies must be guided by a commitment to not harm, promoting fairness, and enhancing the transparency and understanding of AI interventions in health settings. As you navigate the complexities of AI in healthcare, remember that these technologies are not just tools but partners in a shared mission to deliver compassionate, equitable, and effective healthcare solutions across the globe. Your role in this mission is not just about implementing AI but about shaping it to reflect the highest ethical standards, ensuring that it remains firmly rooted in the principles of beneficence and justice for all as healthcare advances.

9.3 AI and Ethical Implications in Global Surveillance

In the contemporary digital age, the application of AI in surveillance activities, both by states and corporations, has grown exponentially. This growth reflects a complex landscape where the drive for security often intersects and occasionally conflicts with the imperative to safeguard personal privacy. Globally, governments employ AI to enhance their surveillance capabilities, aiming to bolster national security and maintain public order. Meanwhile, corporations leverage similar technologies to monitor consumer behavior and improve business operations. However, the extensive reach of AI-enhanced surveillance raises profound ethical questions, necessitating a careful balance between societal safety and individual privacy rights.

The ethical implications of AI in surveillance are multifaceted and global in scope. For instance, in urban settings, AI technologies are increasingly utilized in public surveillance systems to detect anomalies that might indicate criminal activities. While such use can significantly enhance public safety, it also poses risks related to privacy invasion and potential misuse of data. The ethical challenge lies in the collection and storage of vast amounts of data and in the potential for this data to be used in ways that infringe upon individual rights or discriminate against certain groups. This dual aspect of AI surveillance necessitates a nuanced approach where the benefits of enhanced security measures are weighed against the risks of eroding privacy and freedom.

In cities across the globe, from London to Beijing, the deployment of AI surveillance technologies is often justified for security and efficiency. These systems analyze video footage in real-time to identify and respond to perceived threats more swiftly than human operators. However, without stringent safeguards, such technologies can lead to constant surveillance, where every movement is monitored, and personal freedoms can be severely restricted. Therefore, the debate around AI in surveillance often centers on finding the right balance. This pursuit requires robust ethical frameworks and rigorous oversight to ensure that deploying these technologies does not lead to undesirable societal outcomes.

Case Studies of AI Surveillance

Exploring global case studies helps illuminate the diverse ethical landscapes AI surveillance shapes. For example, consider a city implementing AI facial recognition technology in its public transportation system to enhance passenger security. While the system significantly reduced incidents of theft and violence, it also sparked public debates over privacy as travelers' faces were scanned without explicit consent. Another case involved a corporation using AI to monitor employee productivity through computer activities. While this led to efficiency gains, it also led to discomfort and decreased job satisfaction among employees who felt overly scrutinized.

These case studies highlight the societal impacts of AI surveillance, underscoring the need for ethical guidelines that govern its use. They reveal a pattern where the lack of clear ethical standards often leads to public distrust and resistance, which can undermine the very goals that AI surveillance seeks to achieve.

Developing Ethical Guidelines for AI Surveillance

In response to these challenges, there is a pressing need to develop comprehensive ethical guidelines for AI surveillance. These guidelines should prioritize transparency, accountability, and fairness, ensuring that all AI surveillance operations are conducted with respect for human rights. Transparency involves clear communication about what data is collected, how it is used, and who has access to it. Accountability means there are mechanisms to oversee AI surveillance practices and take corrective action if these practices violate ethical standards. Fairness requires that AI systems not exhibit bias that could lead to discrimination against any individual or group.

Moreover, these guidelines should be developed through a participatory process involving policymakers, technologists, civil society, and the general public. This inclusive approach ensures that diverse perspectives and values are considered, leading to more robust and widely accepted ethical standards.

As we conclude this exploration into the ethical dimensions of AI in global surveillance, it becomes clear that while AI has the potential to enhance security and efficiency significantly, it also poses risks that must be carefully managed. Developing and implementing strong ethical guidelines are crucial in ensuring that AI technologies are used responsibly and that their benefits are balanced against the need to protect individual privacy and maintain public trust. This delicate balance is central to ethical AI deployment and the broader goal of ensuring that technological advancements contribute positively to society.

Looking ahead, the next chapter will delve deeper into the ethical considerations of AI in other critical areas, continuing to unravel the complex tapestry of challenges and opportunities that AI presents in our modern world. As we progress, let this discussion serve as a foundation for thoughtful engagement with AI technologies, always mindful of their profound impacts on individuals and societies.

Chapter 10: Ethical Decision-Making in AI Projects

Imagine standing at a crossroads where each path represents a different decision-making framework within artificial intelligence. This chapter is your map, guiding you through the intricate landscapes of ethical frameworks that can steer AI development toward ethical integrity and societal benefit. As an AI professional, understanding and applying these frameworks is not just about compliance; it's about nurturing trust, fostering innovation, and ensuring that the technologies you develop contribute positively to society.

10.1 Frameworks for Ethical Decision-Making in AI

Introduction to Decision-Making Frameworks

Ethical decision-making frameworks serve as vital compasses in the dynamic field of AI, where each decision can ripple through society. These frameworks are not merely academic exercises; they are practical tools that guide developers in navigating the complex ethical terrain of AI. Setting structured guidelines and principles, these frameworks help ensure that AI technologies enhance human welfare without causing unintended harm. For you, the developer, integrating these frameworks into your projects means embedding a layer of ethical foresight into the code and design of AI systems.

Comparative Analysis

When exploring various ethical frameworks specific to AI, it's essential to recognize their diverse origins and focal points. For instance, the Utilitarian Framework emphasizes the greatest good for the greatest number, making it suitable for projects aimed at broad societal benefits, such as AI applications in public health. In contrast, the Deontological Framework focuses on adherence to duties and rules, which ensures that AI respects user privacy and consent irrespective of the outcomes.

Another influential framework is the Virtue Ethics Framework, which encourages AI systems to embody fairness and empathy. This aligns well with AI in education, which aims to foster these virtues in students. Each framework offers unique strengths, and understanding these can help you select the most appropriate one based on your AI project's specific ethical challenges and goals.

Case Application

Consider an AI-driven healthcare diagnostic tool to illustrate the real-world application of these frameworks. Applying the Utilitarian Framework, the development team prioritizes algorithms that improve diagnostic accuracy and treatment outcomes for the largest number of patients. However, they also integrate the Deontological Framework by implementing strict measures to protect patient data privacy, ensuring that the system adheres to ethical obligations of confidentiality and consent.

Another example is an AI-powered recruitment tool designed to minimize hiring biases. Here, the Virtue Ethics Framework guides the development process, focusing on fairness and inclusivity as core functionalities of the AI system. This ensures that the tool performs efficiently and promotes ethical virtues in its operations.

Adapting Frameworks for Specific AI Contexts

While general ethical frameworks provide a solid foundation, the unique challenges of specific AI applications often require customized adaptations. For instance, AI used in autonomous vehicles must address ethical issues related to safety, decision-making in emergencies, and liability. Here, a hybrid framework might be developed, combining utilitarian principles (maximizing safety for all) with deontological rules (e.g., non-discrimination in decision-making).

Customizing these frameworks involves engaging with stakeholders, including technologists, ethicists, and potential users, to understand the specific context and values at stake. It also requires ongoing assessment and iteration to refine the framework as the technology and its societal impacts evolve.

Visual Element: Ethical Framework Comparison Chart

To aid in your decision-making process, below is a chart comparing the key features, strengths, and typical applications of the primary ethical frameworks used in AI. This visual tool is designed to help you quickly assess which framework might be most effective in addressing the ethical dimensions of your specific AI project.

Ethical Framework	Key Features	Strengths	Typical Applications
Utilitarianism	Maximize overall happiness and minimize suffering.	Practical and outcome-focused.	Policy-making, healthcare resource allocation
Deontology	Follow set rules or duties regardless of outcomes	Clear rules and guidelines.	Legal systems corporate ethics.
Virtue Ethics	Focus on moral character and virtues.	Emphasize moral integrity.	Personal Development, leadership.
Ethics of Care	Emphasize relationships and care for others.	Sensitive to context and relationships.	Healthcare, social work.
Fairness and Justice	Ensure fair treatment and equitable outcomes.	Focuses on fairness and equality.	Algorithm fairness, social justice initiatives.
Human Rights Framework	Respects and upholds fundamental human rights (privacy, freedom, equality). Ensures AI systems align with human rights laws and principles.	Strong focus on protecting individual rights. Provides clear, internationally recognized standards	Policy Making Regulatory compliances, Privacy protection in AI.
Consequentialism	Focuses on the outcomes of actions. Considers a broad range of consequences, not just happiness.	Flexible and adaptable to different scenarios. Comprehensive evaluation of impacts.	Assessing societal impacts of AI, Public policy decisions, Environmental impact analysis
Principlism	Combines multiple ethical principles (autonomy, beneficence, non-maleficence, justice). Balances competing ethical considerations.	Holistic approach to ethics. Balances multiple ethical aspects effectively.	Healthcare ethics Biomedical research Complex decision-making scenarios

Figure 7 - Comparison of Key Ethical Frameworks in AI

Why Ethical Frameworks are Important in AI:

- **Guidance**: Provide guidelines for developers, policymakers, and users on ethically designing and implementing AI systems.

- **Accountability**: Help establish accountability for AI decisions and actions, ensuring that ethical considerations are not overlooked.

- **Trust**: Build trust in AI technologies by ensuring they are developed and used in ways that are aligned with societal values and ethical norms.

- **Bias Mitigation**: Address and mitigate biases in AI systems, promoting fairness and equality.

- **Safety**: Ensure that AI systems are safe and do not harm individuals or society.

Challenges Addressed by Ethical Frameworks in AI:

- **Bias and Discrimination**: Ethical frameworks help identify and mitigate biases in AI algorithms that can lead to unfair treatment of individuals or groups.
- **Privacy**: They guide the protection of personal data and ensure that AI systems respect individuals' privacy rights.
- **Autonomy**: Ensure that AI systems support and do not undermine human autonomy and decision-making.
- **Transparency**: Promote transparency and explainability in AI systems, making their operations understandable to users.
- **Accountability**: Establish mechanisms for holding AI developers and users accountable for the ethical implications of their systems.

By applying these ethical frameworks, stakeholders can navigate the complex ethical landscape of AI, making informed decisions that promote the well-being and rights of individuals and society as a whole.

As you continue to navigate the complexities of AI development, remember that choosing and adapting an ethical framework is not a one-time task. It requires continuous engagement, assessment, and adaptation to ensure that your AI projects comply with ethical standards and actively promote the well-being and dignity of all affected by them. This ongoing commitment to ethical decision-making in AI is crucial for your project's success and for advancing AI as a force for good in society.

10.2   Balancing   Innovation   with   Ethical Considerations

In the fast-evolving landscape of artificial intelligence, the sprint toward innovation often finds itself at odds with the methodical pace of ethical deliberation. This tension is not merely academic but a practical challenge you face in developing AI technologies. Balancing rapid technological advances with the imperative for ethical oversight requires a nuanced approach where innovation does not outpace our capacity to understand its implications. Recognizing AI's profound impact on society, your role as a developer transcends technical proficiency, venturing into the realms of ethical stewardship.

The core of this balance lies in understanding that ethical considerations are not just barriers to overcome but are integral components that can enhance the innovation process. They ensure that technologies are effective, fair, transparent, and aligned with societal values. For instance, consider the development of AI in autonomous vehicles. The push for innovation drives the creation of more intelligent, autonomous systems. Still, the ethical imperative demands rigorous testing and fail-safes to ensure these vehicles do not risk public safety. Here, the balance is struck by embedding ethical reviews at each stage of the development process, ensuring that each innovation is matched with commensurate scrutiny regarding its safety and reliability.

Case Studies

Exploring real-world applications, we find successful models in companies that have harmonized innovation with ethical foresight. A notable example is a tech giant renowned for its AI-driven platforms, which established an internal ethics board dedicated to overseeing all AI projects. This board evaluates projects not only for their technological viability but also for their compliance with ethical standards, considering factors such as data privacy, user consent, and potential biases. Through this governance structure, the company ensures that its innovations adhere to ethical guidelines, enhancing user trust and brand reputation.

Another compelling case comes from a startup that developed AI for personalized education. This company implemented a participatory design process involving educators, students, and ethicists. This approach ensured the AI system was tailored to diverse learning needs while respecting ethical concerns about data use and algorithmic transparency. The result was a product that was not only innovative but also ethically attuned, leading to broad acceptance in educational institutions.

Strategies for Maintaining Balance

Several strategies can help navigate this complex landscape. First, it is crucial to integrate ethical considerations into the innovation process from the beginning. This can be achieved through ethical impact assessments, which evaluate the potential effects of AI technologies on various stakeholders. You can design innovative and ethically sound solutions by anticipating issues before they arise.

Another effective strategy is fostering an organizational culture that values ethical considerations as much as technological achievements. This involves regular training for AI teams on ethical issues, encouraging open discussions about ethics, and recognizing efforts to address ethical challenges. Such a culture nurtures compliance with ethical standards and promotes a deeper understanding of how these standards support responsible innovation.

Furthermore, collaboration with external ethicists and interdisciplinary experts can provide fresh perspectives and expertise, helping identify potential ethical issues hidden from those immersed in technology development. These collaborations can lead to more robust and ethically aware AI solutions, enhancing your innovations' societal acceptance and success.

Impact of Balance on AI Advancement

The long-term impacts of prioritizing ethical considerations in AI development are profound. By ensuring that AI technologies are developed with a solid ethical foundation, you contribute to a landscape where society trusts and values innovation. Ethically developed AI systems are more likely to be embraced by users, leading to broader adoption and more significant impact. Moreover, by setting high ethical standards, you help shape industry norms and public expectations, driving the overall field of AI towards more responsible and sustainable practices.

Balancing innovation and ethical oversight is not about compromise but enhancing AI technologies' integrity and impact. As you continue to develop AI solutions, remember that ethical considerations are not just safeguards but are fundamental to the true success of your innovations, ensuring they serve society in just, beneficial, and universally respected ways.

10.3 Ethical Dilemma Case Studies in AI Development

Ethical dilemmas often arise in the intricate world of AI development, challenging developers to navigate complex moral landscapes. These dilemmas from diverse industries provide invaluable learning opportunities and insights that can guide future AI projects. By examining specific cases where ethical challenges were faced and resolved, you gain a deeper understanding of the practical application of ethical principles in AI development.

One poignant example comes from the financial sector, where an AI system designed for loan approval inadvertently favored applicants from specific zip codes. The ethical dilemma centered around unintentional bias, raising significant concerns about fairness and equality. Upon identifying the issue through routine bias testing, the development team embarked on a rigorous analysis to determine the root cause, which was traced back to biased training data that reflected historical lending disparities. The resolution involved retraining the model with a more diverse dataset and implementing regular audits to ensure continued fairness. The lesson here underscores the importance of continuous monitoring and the willingness to recalibrate systems as new ethical insights emerge. For future dilemmas, this case highlights the need for robust data validation processes and the establishment of ongoing ethical audits as part of the AI system's lifecycle.

Another case involved an AI-powered hiring tool used by a multinational corporation, which was reported to show preference towards candidates from certain universities, thereby excluding potentially qualified applicants with different educational backgrounds. This situation presented an ethical dilemma regarding social equity and access to opportunities. The development team initiated a comprehensive decision-making process, incorporating feedback from various stakeholders, including job applicants, HR personnel, and external ethics consultants. The resolution involved adjusting the algorithm to reduce the weight given to educational background and enhancing the system's ability to evaluate diverse experiences and skills. From this, the key lesson learned was the value of stakeholder engagement in identifying and resolving ethical issues, emphasizing that ethical AI development benefits significantly from diverse perspectives and inclusive discussions. Moving forward, guidelines for similar dilemmas should advocate for including a wide range of stakeholder insights during the AI design and review phases.

In the healthcare industry, an AI system designed to schedule patient appointments was found to prioritize patients based on the profitability of their insurance providers rather than medical urgency. This ethical dilemma highlighted justice issues and the prioritization of care based on financial factors rather than patient needs. Upon recognizing this issue, the healthcare provider conducted a thorough analysis involving clinical staff, patients, and AI ethicists to reassess the criteria used by the AI system. The resolution saw the AI being reprogrammed to prioritize medical urgency over financial considerations, aligning the system's operations with the fundamental ethical principle of fairness in healthcare. This case teaches the critical lesson that ethical AI systems must align with sector-specific values, such as prioritizing patient care above financial metrics. For future projects, aligning AI operations with industry ethics is crucial, ensuring systems enhance sectoral practices rather than undermine them.

A final case from the entertainment industry involved an AI algorithm used by a streaming service to recommend movies to users. The algorithm was criticized for promoting content perpetuating stereotypes, leading to an ethical dilemma about cultural representation and reinforcing harmful biases. The team addressed this by analyzing the recommendation patterns and identifying biases in the dataset used to train the AI. They resolved the issue by diversifying the data inputs and adjusting the algorithm to promote a broader range of cultural narratives. The lesson here highlights the impact of AI on cultural perceptions and the responsibility of developers to promote diversity and inclusivity. Future guidelines should emphasize the importance of culturally diverse datasets and the proactive management of content recommendation systems to foster a more inclusive media landscape.

Navigating these ethical dilemmas requires a thoughtful approach, where the implications of AI technologies are continually assessed against robust ethical standards. The lessons from these cases inform better and contribute to a broader understanding of how AI can be developed and deployed responsibly. As we move forward, let these insights inspire more nuanced and ethically aware approaches to AI development, ensuring technologies advance in capability and their capacity to uphold and promote ethical values.

In wrapping up this exploration of ethical dilemmas in AI development, the overarching message is clear: ethical challenges are inherent in developing AI technologies, but they also offer opportunities for growth, learning, and improvement. By studying these dilemmas and their resolutions, you are better equipped to anticipate and address similar challenges in your projects, fostering AI systems that are not only technically proficient but also ethically sound. As we transition to the next chapter, we apply these lessons to ensure AI technologies contribute positively to society, enhancing our capabilities and ethical standards.

Chapter 11: Practical Ethics for AI Developers

In a world where technological advancements surge with the force of a cyclone, the development of artificial intelligence stands as a beacon of both innovation and responsibility. Imagine, if you will, the role of a sculptor, meticulously chiseling away at the marble to reveal the form hidden within. Similarly, as an AI developer, you wield the tools of technology and ethics to craft systems that function efficiently and adhere to the highest standards of moral integrity. Integrating ethics into AI development is not just a supplementary layer—it is the cornerstone of building technology that genuinely benefits humanity.

11.1 Integrating Ethics into the AI Development Process

Ethics from the Start

From the inception of an AI project, ethical considerations must be woven into the fabric of development, just as threads of varying colors and textures come together to form a tapestry. Starting with ethics means more than just compliance or risk management; it means aspiring to create technology that fundamentally respects and enhances human life. This proactive approach ensures that potential ethical issues are identified and addressed before they escalate into more significant problems. For instance, when developing an AI-driven health diagnostic tool, embedding ethics from the start could involve setting clear parameters around data privacy and patient consent, ensuring these critical factors are designed into the system from day one.

Interdisciplinary Teams

The complexity of AI systems and their broad implications across various sectors necessitate the formation of interdisciplinary teams. These teams should include technologists, ethicists, legal experts, sociologists, and representatives from the communities affected by the AI system's deployment. Doing so ensures a holistic view of the technology's impact and a robust approach to ethical considerations. For example, in creating an AI for urban planning, urban sociologists can provide insights into how different communities might interact with or be affected by AI-driven changes, ensuring that the development is both technologically sound and socially responsible.

Checkpoints for Ethical Review

Structuring the development process to include specific checkpoints for ethical review is akin to a pilot performing pre-flight checks. These checkpoints serve as moments to pause and reflect on the ethical dimensions of the AI systems being developed. They should be strategically placed at critical stages of the project, such as before a significant testing phase or before deployment—to assess and ensure compliance with ethical standards. During the development of an AI content recommendation system, checkpoints might include evaluations of algorithm transparency and the potential for unintended bias in content delivery.

Case Examples: Ethical Integration in Practice

One illustrative case of successful ethical integration involves a multinational corporation that developed an AI-powered supply chain system. Recognizing the potential for AI to impact labor markets, the company initiated its project with a comprehensive ethical framework aimed at minimizing job displacement. Interdisciplinary teams, including AI developers, ethical analysts, and employee representatives, collaborated to design a system that optimized the supply chain and retrained employees whose roles were affected by AI automation. This preemptive approach to ethical considerations enhanced the supply chain's efficiency and fostered a positive corporate culture and public image.

Another exemplary project is the development of an AI system for environmental monitoring. The AI was designed to predict areas of high pollution and suggest interventions. Ethical checkpoints were established to assess the interventions' environmental impact and ensure data collection did not infringe on community privacy. These checkpoints helped balance technological efficacy and ethical responsibility, leading to widespread acceptance and support of the project from environmental groups and local communities.

As you continue navigating the complexities of AI development, remember that integrating ethics from the outset is not merely about avoiding harm but actively doing good. By building interdisciplinary teams, establishing regular ethical checkpoints, and learning from successful case studies, you can ensure that your AI projects achieve technical excellence and ethical integrity. This commitment enhances the quality and acceptance of your AI systems and ensures that technology serves as a force for good in society.

11.2 Ethical Auditing of AI Systems

Ethical auditing is a critical safeguard in the fast-paced realm of artificial intelligence, where decisions are made at the speed of data. It is a process designed to ensure that AI systems operate efficiently and with integrity. Ethical auditing comprehensively evaluates AI systems to assess compliance with established ethical standards and regulations. This process is crucial as it helps identify potential ethical issues that could compromise the system's fairness, transparency, and accountability, fostering trust among users and stakeholders.

The purpose of ethical auditing extends beyond mere compliance; it is fundamentally about maintaining the social license to operate. By regularly examining AI systems ethically, developers and companies can mitigate risks, enhance system reliability, and ensure alignment with societal values. The process typically involves several key steps:

- Defining the scope of the audit.

- Identifying relevant ethical standards and regulations.
- Conducting the audit through data analysis and stakeholder interviews.
- Reporting the findings with recommendations for improvement.

Best practices in ethical auditing emphasize thoroughness, transparency, and adaptability. One effective methodology involves ethical matrices, which help map out the potential impacts of AI systems across different stakeholder groups. Tools such as algorithmic impact assessments can provide insights into AI decisions, highlighting areas where biases might occur. Frameworks like the AI Transparency Framework guide auditors in evaluating the comprehensibility and openness of AI systems, ensuring that operations are effective and understandable to those they impact.

Regulatory considerations play a pivotal role in shaping the ethical auditing process. With AI technologies becoming increasingly integral to various sectors—healthcare, finance, education—regulations have evolved to address the unique challenges posed by these technologies. For instance, the GDPR in Europe includes provisions for the right to explanation, where users can ask for the rationale behind AI-driven decisions. This regulation has profound implications for how AI systems are designed and audited, necessitating transparency in algorithmic processes. In the United States, the Algorithmic Accountability Act proposes that companies conduct impact assessments of automated systems to ensure they are free of biases and respect user privacy. These regulations guide the ethical auditing process and elevate the standards to which AI systems are held, promoting societal and ethical responsibility.

To illustrate the practical application of these concepts, consider the case study of an AI-powered recruitment tool developed by a leading tech company. The system was designed to streamline hiring by automatically screening resumes and identifying top candidates. However, concerns arose about the potential for gender bias in the tool's decision-making process. An ethical audit was conducted, involving a review of the algorithm's design, an analysis of the training data, and interviews with the development team and end-users.

The audit revealed that the training data used historical hiring decisions that favored male candidates, replicating these biases in the AI's decisions. The findings prompted immediate action: the training dataset was diversified to include more representative samples, and the algorithm was adjusted to mitigate these biases. Additionally, the company implemented regular ethical reviews as part of the system's lifecycle, ensuring ongoing compliance and improvement.

This case study underscores the importance of ethical audits in identifying and rectifying issues that, if left unchecked, could undermine the fairness and effectiveness of AI systems. It also highlights the dynamic nature of AI ethics, where continuous monitoring and adaptation are necessary to align with evolving societal standards and technological advancements.

As you develop or oversee AI systems, integrating robust ethical auditing processes can be your linchpin in ensuring they are developed and deployed responsibly. This safeguards the interests of users and stakeholders and reinforces the ethical foundation upon which sustainable and trustworthy AI must be built.

11.3 From Development to Deployment: An Ethical Checklist

In crafting AI systems that stand the test of ethical scrutiny, it becomes imperative to have a structured, systematic approach from the beginning of the development process. This approach is embodied in creating a comprehensive ethical checklist as a navigational aid, ensuring every stage of AI development aligns with established ethical standards and practices. Developing such a checklist involves a collaborative effort where insights from various domains—technology, ethics, legal, and societal impact—are amalgamated to form a robust framework. This framework not only streamlines the development process but also embeds a culture of accountability and transparency within the development team.

The critical components of this ethical checklist can be envisioned as the pillars upon which trustworthy AI systems are built. First, data handling, which includes data collection, storage, and usage protocols, ensures data privacy and integrity are always maintained. This component is crucial in building user trust and conforming to global data protection regulations. Second, bias mitigation encompasses strategies and techniques to prevent, identify, and correct biases in AI algorithms and datasets. This is vital for developing fair and inclusive AI systems that do not perpetuate or amplify societal inequalities. Lastly, transparency involves clearly documenting the AI system's design, operation, and decision-making processes. This is essential for user trust and facilitating easier review and accountability in AI operations.

Applying this checklist in practice involves integrating it into every phase of the AI development lifecycle. The checklist guides the design thinking process during the initial conceptualization, ensuring ethical considerations shape the project's objectives and methodologies. For example, when conceptualizing an AI for educational purposes, the checklist would prompt including diverse academic needs and accessibility features right from the start. As the project moves into the development phase, the checklist is a constant reference to ensure all coding, data integration, and algorithm configurations adhere to the ethical standards outlined in the initial stages.

During testing and deployment, the checklist becomes a tool for quality assurance, verifying that the system operates as intended under various scenarios and does not deviate from ethical guidelines. It helps identify any last-minute ethical issues needed before launching the AI system. For instance, in deploying an AI-driven health monitoring tool, the checklist would ensure that the tool does not discriminate against any patient demographics and that all patient data is handled with the utmost confidentiality.

The nature of AI and its interaction with the dynamic human environment necessitates that this ethical checklist is not static but evolves through continuous improvement. Regular updates to the checklist are crucial to adapt to new ethical insights, technological advancements, and changes in regulatory landscapes. This iterative process ensures that the checklist remains relevant and effective in guiding the ethical development of AI systems. Engaging with various stakeholders during these updates brings diverse perspectives, enriching the checklist's comprehensiveness and applicability.

As AI technologies continue to evolve and integrate deeper into societal fabrics, the role of a well-structured ethical checklist becomes increasingly significant. It ensures compliance with ethical standards and fosters a proactive approach to ethical challenges, embedding deep moral considerations into the DNA of AI systems. This proactive engagement with ethics is a cornerstone in building innovative AI technologies that respect human values and rights, paving the way for their acceptance and success in society.

As we conclude this exploration of practical ethics for AI developers, remember that the journey of integrating ethics into AI is continuous and ever-evolving. The strategies and tools we've discussed are not merely checkboxes but foundational elements that enhance the integrity and impact of your AI projects. Looking ahead, the next chapter will delve into public engagement and transparency in AI, exploring how open communication and inclusivity are pivotal in the successful deployment and acceptance of AI technologies. Remember these principles as you forge ahead, ensuring your work advances technology and upholds the highest ethical standards.

Chapter 12: Public Engagement and Transparency in AI

Imagine a world where every technological innovation is like a well-lit room; every corner, every detail is visible, clear, and understood by all who enter. This is the ideal we strive for in the development of artificial intelligence: a scenario where transparency isn't just an option but the foundation upon which trust and understanding between AI developers and the public are built. As you, a pivotal creator and shaper of AI, navigate this landscape, understanding the critical importance of transparency becomes a professional requirement and a moral imperative.

12.1 Strategies for Transparent AI Development

Importance of Transparency

The relationship between transparency and trust is both profound and pivotal. In AI, where decisions can significantly impact lives and societies, the importance of making these processes transparent cannot be overstated. Transparent AI systems allow users and the general public to understand and, crucially, verify the integrity and fairness of the decisions made by these intelligent systems. This openness builds trust and fosters a sense of security and acceptance among those affected by AI technologies. For you, as an AI developer, embedding transparency into your projects means you are not only adhering to ethical standards but are also enhancing the credibility and reliability of your creations.

Mechanisms for Transparency

Achieving transparency in AI development involves a multifaceted approach. One effective mechanism is the adoption of open-source code. By allowing others to view, modify, and distribute your AI source code, you enable peer reviews and collaborative improvements, which enhance the system's reliability and security. Additionally, conducting public audits of AI algorithms is an external validation method, ensuring that the systems operate as intended and adhere to ethical norms. Another critical mechanism is the implementation of transparent data usage policies. These policies should clearly communicate how data is collected, used, and protected, providing assurances and clarity to users about their privacy and data security.

Challenges and Solutions

However, achieving transparency is possible, particularly in competitive commercial environments where proprietary technologies and trade secrets are closely guarded. The challenge here lies in balancing companies' commercial interests with the public's right to transparency. One viable solution is the development of standardized transparency protocols that allow companies to disclose how AI systems operate without revealing proprietary algorithms or data that could compromise their competitive advantage. Another approach uses transparency-enhancing technologies that give users insights into AI decision-making processes without exposing the underlying intellectual property.

Examples of Transparency in Action

To illustrate these concepts, consider the case of a tech company that developed an AI system for personal finance management. The company adopted an open-source approach, allowing independent developers to access and contribute to the system's code. This improved the system's functionality and built a community of trust and collaboration around the product. The company complemented this with robust data usage policies that transparently communicated to users, explaining how their financial data was processed and protected. This approach complied with regulatory standards and significantly enhanced user trust and engagement.

Furthermore, a university deployed an AI system to personalize learning experiences in an educational initiative. An independent body regularly audited the system's algorithms and published the results publicly. This transparency in auditing procedures reassured students and educators of the system's fairness and accuracy, leading to broader acceptance and use of the technology in educational settings.

As you continue to develop and deploy AI systems, remember that the journey toward transparency is continuous and requires constant vigilance and adaptation. By implementing these strategies and learning from successful examples, you can ensure that your AI projects are technologically advanced, ethically sound, and publicly trusted. This commitment to transparency enhances the quality of your AI systems. It contributes to the broader goal of fostering an informed and engaged public that actively participates in the AI landscape.

12.2 Public Perception of AI Ethics

Public perception of artificial intelligence and its ethical implications remains a kaleidoscope of concerns and expectations, reflecting a broad spectrum of societal viewpoints. Among the most pressing issues is the concern over privacy, with many fearing that AI technologies might lead to unprecedented surveillance and data breaches. Equally, the anxiety around job displacement due to AI automation is palpable across various industries. Furthermore, the question of decision-making autonomy—how much control AI should have over critical decisions and the transparency of such decisions continues to provoke significant debate. These concerns are theoretical; they shape public attitudes toward AI and can significantly influence its adoption and development.

To navigate these concerns, a proactive approach is required—one that not only addresses these worries but also works to shape a more informed and positive public perception of AI ethics. Initiatives such as targeted education campaigns play a crucial role in this. By demystifying AI technologies and clarifying their ethical dimensions, these campaigns can alleviate misconceptions and build a more nuanced understanding of AI's potential and limitations. For instance, educational programs that explain how AI systems make decisions, the measures in place to protect data, and how AI can potentially create new job opportunities rather than merely erase existing ones can help reshape public perceptions to be more reflective of AI's realistic impact.

Public dialogues also serve as a vital platform for shaping perceptions. By fostering discussions involving a broad range of participants; tech developers, ethicists, the general public, and policymakers—these dialogues ensure diverse perspectives on AI ethics are heard and considered. This inclusivity enriches the conversation and enhances the community's engagement with AI ethics, making the technology's development and implementation more democratic and socially informed.

The impact of public perception on AI development must be considered. A positive public outlook on AI can accelerate its adoption across sectors, while a negative perception can lead to stringent regulations that might stifle innovation. Therefore, the development trajectory of AI technologies is closely tied to how well public concerns are understood and addressed. It becomes imperative for developers to not only focus on advancing AI technology but also on advancing the public's understanding and trust in these systems.

Several case studies highlight how public perception has directly influenced AI projects. One notable example involves a major tech company that introduced a chatbot designed to learn from daily user interactions. However, without sufficient safeguards, the chatbot quickly started producing offensive content, reflecting some of the darker aspects of human interactions it learned from online. The public backlash was swift and severe, with concerns about ethical oversight and content moderation. The company had to pull down the chatbot and reassess its deployment strategy, focusing more on ethical safeguards and the system's ability to reject harmful inputs. This incident changed the company's approach to AI development and served as a cautionary tale about the importance of ethical considerations in AI deployment.

In another instance, a city's proposal to implement AI-powered facial recognition technology for public surveillance was met with significant public opposition. Citizens expressed concerns over privacy infringement and the potential for racial profiling. In response, city officials organized a series of public forums and workshops to discuss these concerns. The outcome was a decision to implement strict regulations on the use of the technology, including clear guidelines on data handling, consent protocols, and an oversight committee to monitor its use. This case highlights how public input can lead to more ethically sound and publicly accepted AI applications.

As AI continues to evolve and integrate more profoundly into society's fabric, understanding and shaping public perception through education and open dialogue remains crucial. By engaging with the public's concerns and fostering an informed discourse, you can help ensure that AI development advances technologically and does so with the ethical rigor and public support essential for its long-term success.

12.3 Engaging with Stakeholders on AI Ethics

In the complex ecosystem of artificial intelligence development, understanding and engaging with key stakeholders is not just beneficial; ensuring that AI technologies are ethically sound and socially acceptable is imperative. Stakeholders in AI development encompass a broad spectrum of individuals and groups, each bringing unique perspectives and values to the table. End-users, the direct recipients of AI technology, offer insights into AI systems' usability and real-world implications. Communities affected by AI deployment can provide valuable feedback on social impacts and ethical concerns. Regulators and policymakers play a crucial role in setting the legal and ethical frameworks within which AI operates, while advocacy groups often highlight ethical issues and represent marginalized voices. Together, these stakeholders form a comprehensive network of influences that can significantly shape the direction and success of AI projects.

Engaging with these diverse stakeholders requires a strategic and inclusive approach. Collaborative workshops are powerful for bringing different stakeholders together, facilitating a shared understanding, and collective brainstorming on ethical AI development. These workshops can be structured to allow stakeholders to express their concerns, propose solutions, and directly interact with the developers, fostering a sense of collaboration and mutual respect. Feedback mechanisms such as surveys, focus groups, and online forums also play a critical role. They provide stakeholders with ongoing opportunities to influence AI projects, ensuring that their input is not limited to a one-time event but is integrated throughout the AI development lifecycle. Additionally, establishing stakeholder advisory boards can provide continuous guidance and oversight, offering expert insights and ethical oversight from diverse voices.

The benefits of robust stakeholder engagement are manifold. Firstly, it enhances trust between AI developers and the community. When stakeholders see that their input is valued and reflected in the development process, it builds confidence in the AI systems being developed. This trust is crucial not only for adopting new technologies but also for the long-term reputation of AI firms. Furthermore, engagement leads to better-informed ethical considerations. By incorporating diverse perspectives, AI developers can foresee potential ethical issues that might not be apparent from a purely technical viewpoint, allowing for more comprehensive and proactive ethical planning. Moreover, the social acceptance of AI projects is markedly increased when stakeholders feel they have a voice in the development process. This social buy-in is essential for successfully integrating AI technologies into everyday lives.

Successful examples of stakeholder engagement in AI abound, illustrating the positive outcomes of these strategies. One notable instance involved a city council deploying an AI system to manage public transportation. The project team gathered insights by organizing collaborative workshops with commuters, city planners, and traffic management officials. This led to an AI solution that optimized traffic flow without compromising public safety or convenience. The feedback mechanisms established allowed for ongoing suggestions, which kept the system adaptive to changing traffic patterns and user needs, thereby maintaining high levels of public approval and satisfaction.

Another example comes from a healthcare AI project designed to assist in patient diagnosis. The development team formed an advisory board that included medical professionals, patient advocacy groups, and AI ethics experts. This board met regularly to review the AI's diagnostic processes, ensuring they aligned with ethical healthcare practices and respected patient rights. Including diverse healthcare stakeholders improved the AI's diagnostic accuracy. They ensured that the system adhered to the highest standards of patient care and confidentiality, earning trust from healthcare providers and patients.

Effective stakeholder engagement becomes increasingly critical as AI evolves and becomes more integrated into societal frameworks. By adopting inclusive strategies and recognizing the invaluable insights that diverse groups bring, you can ensure that your AI projects are technologically advanced, ethically robust, and widely accepted. This commitment to inclusive development is not merely a good practice—it's a cornerstone of building AI solutions that genuinely benefit society.

In wrapping up this chapter on public engagement and transparency in AI, we've navigated through the strategies and benefits of maintaining openness and fostering dialogue with the community and stakeholders involved in or affected by AI technologies. Engaging deeply with these groups ensures that a broad spectrum of ethical considerations guides AI development and enjoys robust social support. As we move forward, these engagement and transparency practices build trust and pave the way for AI technologies that are embraced for their ethical integrity and societal value. Looking ahead, the next chapter will delve into the future challenges and opportunities in AI ethics, exploring how ongoing developments might shape our approach to ethical AI in the coming years.

Chapter 13: Anticiating Future Ethical Challenges in AI

As you stand on the precipice of the next wave of artificial intelligence advancements, it's vital to cast your gaze on the horizons of technological innovation and the shadow it casts upon ethical landscapes. The rapid evolution of AI technologies, like quantum computing and autonomous decision-making systems, brings a cascade of ethical challenges that are as complex as they are critical to address. This chapter delves into these emerging ethical issues, exploring the nuanced implications these technologies may have on society, governance, and even the fabric of human morality and safety.

13.1 Emerging Ethical Issues in AI

Imagine a world where decision-making can be outsourced to machines that operate at quantum speeds, capable of processing volumes of data that are unfathomable to the human mind. Quantum computing promises to elevate AI's capabilities, making current technologies look primitive. However, this quantum leap also introduces profound ethical dilemmas. The power of quantum-enhanced AI could lead to breakthroughs in medicine and science but also poses significant risks if these systems make decisions that are not fully transparent or understandable to humans. How do we ensure accountability when decisions are made at speeds and complexities that exceed human comprehension?

Moreover, the autonomy granted to AI systems in decision-making processes heralds a new era of efficiency and precision but brings a host of ethical concerns. Autonomous AI systems, from self-driving cars to autonomous weapons, must be governed by ethical frameworks prioritizing human safety and moral values. Yet, delegating critical decisions to AI raises pivotal questions about the erosion of human control and the potential for AI systems to operate outside of intended ethical boundaries. As you develop these systems, you must balance leveraging autonomous capabilities and maintaining stringent ethical oversight.

Turning to military applications, the use of AI in warfare exemplifies the dual-use nature of technology. On the one hand, AI can optimize defense strategies and reduce human casualties in conflict zones. Conversely, there's the terrifying prospect of autonomous weapons making life-and-death decisions without human intervention. The ethical implications are vast and deeply concerning, necessitating a robust international regulatory framework to govern the use of AI in military settings. Such regulations must be crafted not only to safeguard human rights but also with the foresight to prevent an arms race in autonomous weaponry.

Visual Element: Infographic on AI in Warfare

The infographic starkly visualizes AI's potential uses and abuses in military contexts, illustrating the need for stringent global controls and ethical guidelines.

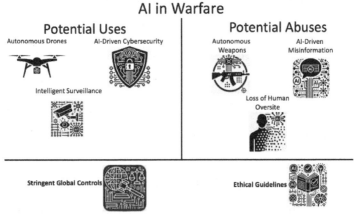

Figure 8 - AI in Warfare

Key Sections of the Infographic:

1. **Potential Uses of AI in Warfare:**

   o **Autonomous Drones**: AI-driven drones for surveillance and targeted operations. The drone icon represents this.

   o **AI-Driven Cybersecurity**: Advanced AI systems to protect against cyber threats. This icon features elements such as a shield, a lock, and a network-related symbol.

   o **Intelligent Surveillance**: Enhanced surveillance capabilities using AI to monitor and analyze data. This icon features elements such as a camera, an eye, and a network-related symbol.

2. **Potential Abuses of AI in Warfare:**

   o **Autonomous Weapons**: AI-powered weapons that can make lethal decisions without human intervention. This is represented by an icon featuring a weapon integrated with AI technology, like a neural network or circuit symbol.

   o **AI-Driven Misinformation**: Using AI to spread false information and propaganda. This is represented by an icon featuring a speech bubble with misleading information and an AI-related symbol.

- o **Loss of Human Oversight**: Diminished human control over AI decisions in critical military operations. This is represented by an icon featuring a human figure overshadowed by AI elements like a neural network or circuit.

3. **Need for Stringent Global Controls and Ethical Guidelines:**

- o Emphasizes the importance of establishing global regulations to control the use of AI in warfare. The icon features a globe, scales of justice, and AI-related symbols to convey the concept of global governance and regulation of AI technologies in military contexts.

- o This icon highlights the necessity of ethical guidelines to ensure AI technologies are used responsibly and do not lead to unintended consequences. It features elements such as an open book or document, a lightbulb for responsibility, and AI-related symbols.

Lastly, the specter of superintelligence, AI systems that might surpass human intelligence, looms large. While the development of superintelligent AI offers unimaginable benefits, such as solving complex global challenges, it poses existential risks that could threaten humanity's existence. The control problem, or the challenge of ensuring that superintelligent systems do not act against human interests, is paramount. Furthermore, alignment issues, ensuring AI's goals are deeply congruent with human values, present significant technical and ethical hurdles. These challenges are not just theoretical; they demand urgent attention and preemptive solutions to mitigate risks that could arise from creating entities whose intelligence dwarfs our own.

As you engage with these advanced AI technologies, remember that the ethical landscapes they touch are as intricate and expansive as their potential applications. As developers and ethicists, you must build or oversee these technologies and shepherd them into existence with a deep commitment to ethical integrity and human values. This stewardship is essential for upholding moral standards and ensuring the long-term sustainability and acceptance of AI technologies in society.

13.2 Long-Term Ethical Considerations in AI Development

In contemplating the future landscape of artificial intelligence, it becomes essential to consider the sustainability of AI technologies, not merely from a technological standpoint but through the lens of environmental ethics and resource stewardship. As AI systems become more ubiquitous, their impact on the environment and resource consumption becomes a pressing ethical concern. For instance, the energy-intensive nature of training complex AI models has already raised significant environmental concerns. The carbon footprint associated with powering AI is immense, especially as the demand for more sophisticated models grows. This situation beckons a shift towards developing more energy-efficient AI algorithms and adopting renewable energy sources in data centers that power AI computations. In addition, the lifecycle of AI hardware—often characterized by rapid obsolescence and a heavy reliance on rare earth minerals—calls for reevaluating resource circularity and sustainability in manufacturing practices. Your role as developers and ethicists is pivotal in driving the adoption of green AI practices that prioritize long-term environmental sustainability over short-term gains.

Turning to the societal impacts of AI, one of the most profound concerns is how these technologies might exacerbate or alleviate economic disparities. AI has the potential to significantly disrupt global labor markets, automate jobs, and shift economic power structures, potentially widening the gap between the economically privileged and underprivileged. This disruption presents an ethical imperative to steer AI development towards reducing economic disparities rather than exacerbating them. For instance, by designing AI technologies that enhance educational access and quality for underprivileged communities, you can help level the playing field and build a more equitable economic future. Moreover, AI can be pivotal in providing low-cost healthcare solutions in economically disadvantaged regions, thus improving health outcomes and economic productivity. However, this also requires vigilant regulation and ethical guidelines to ensure that AI deployment in financially sensitive areas is done with the utmost consideration for the local population's welfare and without exploitative practices.

Preserving human dignity in the realm of AI is another cornerstone of ethical AI development. As AI increasingly interfaces with aspects of daily life, from personal care robots in healthcare to AI-driven decision-making in employment, ensuring these technologies respect and enhance human dignity becomes paramount. In healthcare, AI applications must be developed with an evident ethic of care, ensuring they supplement rather than supplant the human touch, particularly in sensitive areas such as elder care or mental health. AI tools should support employee development and well-being in the workplace, not just for monitoring and evaluation purposes. Ensuring that AI respects human dignity involves:

- Embedding ethical considerations into the design and deployment of AI systems.
- Promoting transparency.
- Ensuring fairness.
- Fostering an environment where AI supports human capabilities and freedoms rather than diminishes them.

Lastly, the role of AI in shaping future societies is both an exciting and daunting prospect. As AI technologies become embedded in society's cultural and social fabric, they will inevitably influence aspects of human identity and societal norms. For example, as generative AI begins to produce art, music, and literature, it will define cultural trends and aesthetic values. Furthermore, AI-driven social media algorithms have the power to shape political opinions and social interactions. This influence casts a profound responsibility on AI developers and regulators to ensure that these technologies are deployed in ways that positively shape societal norms and support democratic values. The potential of AI to redefine aspects of human identity and culture must be approached with a careful blend of innovation enthusiasm and ethical prudence.

As you navigate these complex ethical territories, remember that the decisions you make today will echo in tomorrow's societal and environmental landscapes. The development of AI is not just a technical challenge but a profound ethical endeavor that requires a deep commitment to the long-term consequences of these powerful technologies.

13.3 Preparing for the Unpredictable: An Ethical Framework

In the dynamic realm of AI, where the only constant is change, developing adaptive ethical frameworks is akin to constructing a building designed to withstand earthquakes—it must be robust yet flexible enough to adapt to unforeseen shifts. As you, the vanguards of AI development, continue to push the boundaries of what machines can do, it becomes imperative to ensure that your ethical frameworks are not static relics but living systems that evolve alongside technological advancements and societal shifts. This evolution is crucial for maintaining relevance and addressing new ethical challenges that emerge as AI becomes more integrated into every aspect of human life.

The concept of adaptive ethical frameworks involves a continuous process of assessment, update, and integration. These frameworks should be designed with mechanisms that allow for regular updates based on new research, technological developments, and societal feedback. For instance, consider an AI system designed for predictive policing. As societal norms and laws evolve, so should the ethical guidelines governing such systems, ensuring they remain just and effective without infringing on civil liberties. Developing these frameworks should involve a broad spectrum of stakeholders—ethicists, technologists, legal experts, and representatives from affected communities—to ensure a comprehensive understanding of the ethical implications from multiple perspectives.

Flexibility and resilience are the bedrock upon which these adaptive frameworks must be built. Flexibility in ethical frameworks allows for the swift incorporation of new findings and technologies without overhauling the entire system. This flexibility might manifest in modular ethics policies that can be updated independently without affecting the framework's integrity. Resilience is equally essential, ensuring that ethical frameworks can withstand challenges and pressures from rapid technological advancements and critical societal changes. This resilience can be fostered through stress-testing frameworks under various hypothetical scenarios to identify potential weaknesses and areas for improvement.

Moreover, incorporating ethical risk assessment models plays a pivotal role in anticipating and mitigating potential ethical issues before they manifest in real-world applications. Similar to the predictive models used in finance to forecast market risks, these models can analyze vast amounts of data from existing AI systems to predict where ethical breaches might occur. For example, by analyzing data from social media algorithms, risk assessment models could predict potential biases or privacy issues, allowing developers to address these issues proactively. Implementing these models as standard practice in AI development processes ensures a preemptive approach to ethics, reducing the likelihood of harm and increasing trust in AI applications.

Global collaboration is essential for crafting comprehensive and universally applicable ethical frameworks. In a world where AI technologies easily cross borders, international cooperation ensures that ethical standards are consistent and that global diversity is respected. This collaboration can take many forms, from international conferences and workshops that set global ethical guidelines to cross-border research initiatives that explore cultural differences in ethical perceptions of AI. For instance, a global consortium on AI ethics could facilitate the sharing of best practices and success stories, fostering a collaborative environment where innovations in ethical AI are celebrated and emulated worldwide.

Navigating the unpredictable requires a detailed and adaptable map. In the landscape of AI, this map is your ethical framework. By ensuring these frameworks are adaptive, flexible, resilient, and internationally collaborative, you are better equipped to face whatever new challenges and opportunities AI might bring. This proactive approach safeguards against potential ethical pitfalls. It ensures that AI development is conducted under the highest ethical standards, promoting a future where AI contributes positively to global societal and technological progress.

As this chapter closes, we reflect on the indispensable role of adaptive ethical frameworks in the continuing evolution of AI. The insights and strategies discussed here are crucial for preparing AI development to meet future ethical challenges head-on. As we turn the page, the next chapter will delve deeper into innovative strategies for ethical AI development, ensuring that as AI technologies advance, they do so with integrity and respect for the broad spectrum of human values.

Chapter 14: Innovation and Ethics in AI Development

As dawn breaks over the horizon of artificial intelligence, its rays illuminate a landscape where innovation and ethics intersect, challenging you, the AI developer, to tread a path that upholds the greater good while pushing the boundaries of what machines can achieve. This chapter delves into the essence of innovating responsibly, where ethical considerations are not mere afterthoughts but integral components of the AI development process. Here, we explore how embedding ethical standards into the fabric of AI innovation can catalyze advancements that are not only technologically profound but also socially beneficial and universally trusted.

14.1 Innovating Responsibly with AI

Principles of Responsible Innovation

Responsible innovation in the realm of AI is akin to a seasoned navigator charting a course through unexplored territories. It requires you to be acutely aware of the potential impacts of AI technologies, both intended and unintended. The principles of responsible innovation serve as your compass, guiding your efforts to ensure AI development is conducted with foresight, transparency, and accountability. These principles emphasize the importance of inclusivity, involving diverse stakeholders in the AI development process to gather a multitude of perspectives and ethical considerations. They also stress the necessity of anticipation, encouraging you to look beyond immediate technological achievements to consider long-term impacts on society and the environment. Furthermore, reflexivity requires you to continually assess and re-evaluate the ethical implications of your work, adapting and evolving your approach in response to new information and societal feedback. Lastly, responsiveness highlights the need to act swiftly to mitigate any adverse consequences or ethical issues arising during AI technology development and deployment.

Balancing Speed and Ethics

Finding a balance is crucial in the fast-paced world of AI development, where the pressure to innovate quickly can often overshadow the need for careful ethical consideration. Maintaining this balance involves embedding ethical checkpoints throughout the development process, where AI projects are evaluated against ethical standards at multiple stages. This structured approach ensures that ethical deliberations keep pace with technological advancements. Additionally, fostering a culture within AI teams that values ethical considerations as much as technical achievements can shift the overall focus toward more responsible innovation. This cultural shift can be supported by leadership that champions ethical standards and provides ongoing ethics training to keep all team members informed and engaged.

Ethics as a Driver of Innovation

Contrary to the common perception that ethical considerations might stifle innovation, they can serve as a catalyst for more creative and impactful AI solutions. By framing ethics as a fundamental aspect of the innovation process, you open up new avenues for technological advancement. Ethical challenges encourage you to think more deeply and creatively about how to solve problems in beneficial and just ways. For instance, the challenge of developing AI systems that perform equally well across diverse demographic groups can lead to breakthroughs in data processing and algorithm design. These advancements enhance AI applications' fairness, robustness, and generalizability, making them more effective and reliable in various real-world settings.

Industry Best Practices

Drawing on the experiences of leading tech companies that have successfully integrated ethics into their AI innovation processes can provide valuable insights and models for responsible AI development. These companies often employ comprehensive ethics policies and have dedicated teams responsible for ensuring these policies are followed throughout the AI lifecycle. For example, a prominent technology firm has established an AI ethics board that reviews all new projects to ensure they align with established ethical guidelines. Another best practice is the use of transparency reports, where companies regularly publish details about their AI systems' performance, including any issues of bias or fairness, fostering trust and accountability with users and regulators alike.

As you continue to navigate the complexities of AI development, let the principles of responsible innovation light your way. These principles will ensure that your technological creations reach new heights of capability and embody the highest standards of ethical integrity. By embracing these principles, you contribute to a future where AI technologies are robust, innovative, and deeply aligned with society's values and needs.

14.2 Case Studies: Ethical Innovation in AI

In the evolving tapestry of artificial intelligence, the integration of ethical principles is not merely a regulatory necessity but a cornerstone for genuine innovation and societal benefit. This ethos is vividly reflected in several AI projects tailored for social good, where the commitment to ethical principles has guided technological development and ensured these innovations achieve meaningful and sustainable impacts. An AI-driven initiative to enhance agricultural yields in underdeveloped regions is a particularly compelling example. AI technologies were employed to analyze soil health and weather patterns to provide small-scale farmers with actionable insights tailored to their specific environmental conditions. Ethical considerations were paramount, involving local communities in the data collection to ensure transparency and respect for local practices. This approach improved crop yields and empowered communities with knowledge, fostering long-term agricultural sustainability.

Navigating ethical hurdles is another critical aspect in which AI developers have shown resilience and innovation. Consider the development of an AI system designed to assist in mental health diagnosis. The initial prototypes, although technically proficient, raised significant ethical concerns regarding privacy and the potential misuse of sensitive data. The development team, recognizing these issues, engaged with healthcare professionals, ethicists, and patient advocacy groups to redesign the system. This collaborative effort led to the implementation of robust data encryption and strict access controls, ensuring patient confidentiality. Moreover, the system was adjusted to provide users with clear explanations of how their data would be used, enhancing transparency and trust. This case highlights the challenges encountered and the thoughtful solutions implemented to align AI development with ethical standards.

However, the path of ethical AI development is full of missteps. A notable example involves an AI project to automate the screening process for job applicants. Despite its intention to streamline hiring, the AI system inadvertently perpetuated existing biases, favoring candidates from certain demographic groups. This failure prompted a significant backlash, leading to a reevaluation of the project. The lessons learned were invaluable. The company revised its data sets to eliminate historical biases and introduced ongoing bias monitoring systems to assess and adjust the AI's decision-making processes continually.

This experience underscored the importance of vigilance and continuous improvement in AI development to prevent and rectify ethical oversights.

Pioneering companies in ethical AI innovation offer further insights into the successful integration of ethics into AI development. One such company has made significant strides in developing AI for healthcare, with a strong focus on ethical transparency and patient-centered design. Their strategy involves rigorous testing phases that assess the AI's medical accuracy and adherence to ethical standards, including patient privacy and consent. Challenges, such as ensuring the AI's recommendations are explainable and justifiable to medical professionals, are met with innovative solutions like incorporating explainability features that allow healthcare providers to understand the AI's reasoning process. The achievements of this company demonstrate how a steadfast commitment to ethics can drive technological advancements that are both innovative and aligned with the highest standards of care and respect for individual rights.

In your role as AI developers, ethicists, end users, and others, these case studies provide rich knowledge and inspiration. They illustrate how ethical challenges, when approached with commitment and creativity, can lead to advancements that push the boundaries of what AI can achieve and ensure these technologies contribute positively to society. As you continue to navigate the complex interplay between innovation and ethics in AI development, let these examples serve as beacons, guiding your efforts to create AI solutions that are not only effective but also deeply rooted in ethical integrity and social responsibility.

14.3 Future-Proofing AI Technologies Through Ethics

In the rapidly evolving landscape of artificial intelligence, the concept of "future-proofing" takes on a critical role, particularly from an ethical perspective. Embedding ethics directly into the AI design and development process is akin to weaving a solid moral fiber into the fabric of AI technologies. This proactive approach ensures that AI systems inherently uphold ethical standards as they evolve, reducing the risk of unintended consequences arising from their interactions with humans and their environments.

Effectively embedding ethics into AI design begins with the integration of ethical considerations at the very inception of a project. This means ethical impact assessments are conducted during the initial design phase, not as an afterthought. Doing this lets you identify potential ethical risks and design strategies to mitigate them immediately. For instance, if an AI system is being developed to handle personal data, embedding data protection features directly into the system's architecture can be planned from the outset. This could involve designing algorithms that inherently anonymize data, thus preserving user privacy by default. Another method is the use of ethical guidelines as design constraints. AI systems are programmed to operate within predefined ethical boundaries, such as ensuring fairness by avoiding biased data or implementing fail-safes that prevent AI from making unethically high-risk decisions.

The role of regulations and policies in future-proofing AI technologies against ethical risks cannot be overstated. Regulations serve as a guiding framework within which AI technologies must operate, ensuring a baseline level of ethical compliance. However, the dynamic nature of AI technology often needs to improve the formulation of relevant policies, posing a challenge to effective regulation. To address this, there is a growing need for dynamic regulatory frameworks that can adapt to technological advancements without stifling innovation. These frameworks should facilitate ongoing dialogue between regulators and AI developers, enabling a responsive regulatory environment that evolves in tandem with AI technologies. Moreover, international cooperation in policy formulation can help create a unified global standard for AI ethics, addressing cross-border ethical issues more effectively.

Ethics by Design Case Examples

Illustrating the effectiveness of the ethics by design approach, consider the development of an AI-driven platform used to recommend educational content to students. The platform was designed with ethical considerations, explicitly focusing on ensuring fairness and avoiding biases affecting recommendations based on gender, ethnicity, or socioeconomic status. Techniques used included the implementation of algorithms that regularly audit and adjust the criteria used for content recommendations to ensure they remain fair and inclusive. Additionally, the system was equipped with transparency features, allowing users to see the reasons behind specific recommendations, thus fostering trust and understanding.

Another example is an AI system developed for hiring processes. The system was designed to eliminate gender and ethnic biases typically found in traditional hiring. This was achieved using algorithms trained on diverse datasets and tested for bias across various demographic groups. The developers also implemented a continuous feedback loop, where the AI system's decisions are regularly reviewed and recalibrated if any biases are detected. This approach not only improved the fairness of the hiring process but also enhanced the company's reputation and compliance with employment laws.

Long-Term Ethical Planning

Advocating for incorporating long-term ethical planning in AI development underscores the importance of sustainability in AI ethics. Long-term planning involves anticipating future ethical challenges and proactively developing strategies to address them. This could mean designing AI systems that can adapt their ethical parameters in response to societal norms or technological capabilities changes. For instance, an AI system initially programmed to adhere to specific privacy standards may need to adjust these standards as legal definitions of privacy evolve. Implementing mechanisms for regular ethical audits and updates can ensure that AI systems remain aligned with both current and future ethical standards.

Moreover, long-term ethical planning emphasizes the importance of ongoing evaluation and adaptation. It recognizes that as AI technologies become more integrated into society, their long-term impacts, which may take time to be apparent, must be continually assessed. This ongoing evaluation helps identify new ethical issues as they arise and develop appropriate responses to them. Such a strategy helps mitigate risks and harness opportunities for positive societal impacts, ensuring that AI technologies contribute constructively to human progress.

In wrapping up this exploration of future-proofing AI technologies through ethics, we've seen how embedding ethics into AI design, aligning with dynamic regulatory frameworks, and planning for the long term are crucial for developing AI technologies that are not only innovative but also ethically responsible. As we move forward, these practices will be pivotal in shaping AI systems that are trusted and beneficial across all sectors of society. The next chapter will build on these ideas, focusing on specific strategies for ethical implementation in various AI applications, providing you with practical tools and insights to apply in your own AI projects.

Chapter 15: Building Ethical AI Teams

15.1 The Importance of Diversity in AI Development Teams

Imagine standing before a tapestry woven from threads of myriad colors and textures, each contributing to a vibrant and coherent whole. This image aptly symbolizes the essence of diversity in AI development teams. In a field as dynamic and impactful as artificial intelligence, the confluence of varied human experiences and perspectives isn't just beneficial; it's imperative for fostering innovation and crafting AI systems that are fair, unbiased, and truly reflective of the diverse world they serve.

Diversity and Innovation: Diversity within AI development teams is a powerful catalyst for innovation. When you bring together individuals from different cultural, educational, or experiential backgrounds, you create a melting pot of ideas that can challenge conventional thinking and spur creativity. This variety allows for a broader range of problem-solving approaches, which is crucial in a field as complex as AI. For instance, diverse teams are more likely to identify and address potential biases in AI algorithms that might not be evident to a more homogenous group. This capability to foresee and mitigate issues enhances the robustness of AI systems and ensures they operate equitably across diverse populations.

Overcoming Homogeneity Challenges: Despite the clear advantages of diversity, the tech industry often grapples with homogeneity, particularly regarding gender and ethnicity. This uniformity can stifle innovation and lead to AI systems that inadvertently perpetuate existing biases. Overcoming this challenge requires intentional strategies. Firstly, recruitment practices must be reevaluated. Traditional hiring methods that rely heavily on referrals or pedigrees from certain institutions can perpetuate homogeneity. Expanding recruitment channels, implementing blind hiring practices, and setting diversity targets can help to assemble a more varied workforce. Additionally, fostering an inclusive company culture is essential. This means creating environments where all employees feel valued and safe to express their unique perspectives and ideas without fear of discrimination or tokenism.

Benefits of Diverse Perspectives: Incorporating diverse perspectives in AI development extends beyond enhancing creativity and problem-solving. Teams that are diverse in gender, race, age, and more can better understand and anticipate the needs of a global user base, leading to products that are accessible and useful to a broader audience. Moreover, such teams can navigate cultural nuances more adeptly, which is crucial when deploying AI systems in different parts of the world. For example, an AI application developed for education that considers diverse cultural perspectives on learning styles and educational values is more likely to gain widespread acceptance and effectiveness.

Success Stories: Numerous organizations have recognized diversity's value and reaped substantial benefits. Consider the case of a global tech company that revamped its AI development team by integrating members from six continents. This team successfully developed a translation tool that outperformed existing applications due to its nuanced understanding of linguistic subtleties informed by the team's diverse backgrounds. Another success story involves a startup that developed an AI-driven hiring tool to reduce unconscious bias in recruitment processes. By employing a diverse development team, the company could ensure that its AI system accounted for various hiring biases, making the tool popular among corporations striving to improve their diversity and inclusion.

Visual Element: Infographic on Diversity in AI Innovation

This infographic illustrates vital statistics highlighting the correlation between diverse AI teams and increased innovation. It showcases examples of AI applications improved by diverse developer inputs and serves as a visual affirmation of the power of inclusivity in driving technological advancement.

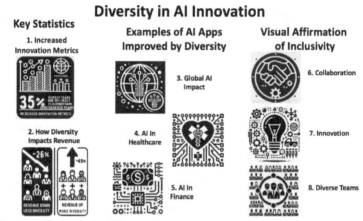

Figure 9 - Diversity in AI Innovation

Infographic Description: Diversity in AI Innovation

Key Statistics Section:

1. **Increased Innovation Metrics:** This icon represents a bar chart showing increased innovation metrics. Typically, diverse teams are 35% more likely to outperform homogeneous teams.

   - Gender-diverse companies are 21% more likely to outperform.
   - Ethnically diverse companies are 33% more likely to outperform.
   - Non-diverse companies are 29% more likely to *underperform.*

2. **Diversity vs. Revenue:** This icon demonstrates diversity because companies with higher diversity scores report 19% higher revenue.

   - Companies with below-average diversity earned 26% of their revenue from innovation.
   - Companies with above-average diversity earned 45% of revenue from innovation.
   - Businesses with more diverse management teams have 19% *higher* revenue due to innovation.

Examples of AI Applications Improved by Diverse Inputs:

3. **Global AI Impact:** This represents a globe symbolizing global AI impact, featuring a globe with elements of AI, such as a neural network or circuit integrated into it.

4. **Healthcare AI:** This represents healthcare AI, featuring a medical symbol combined with AI elements like a neural network or circuit. The medical symbol highlights healthcare AI. To improve medical diagnosis, having a culturally diverse team creates more inclusive health solutions.

5. **AI in Finance:** This represents AI in finance, featuring a financial symbol combined with AI elements like a neural network or circuit. Varied perspectives improve risk assessments and predictions.

Visual Affirmation of Inclusivity:

6. **Collaboration:** This icon represents collaboration, featuring a handshake. Diverse teams make better and faster decisions.

- They make decisions 2X faster with ½ the number of meetings.
- And their decisions deliver 60% better results.
- Why? They focus more on facts.

7. **Innovation:** This represents innovation, featuring a lightbulb. Diverse teams are more innovative. Inclusivity drives technological advancements and thrives in diverse environments.

8. **Diverse Teams:** This represents a team with a diverse composition featuring multiple human figures to symbolize diversity and teamwork. Diverse developer teams create more robust AI solutions, and employees want more diversity and inclusion at work.

- 67% of job seekers said a diverse workforce is essential when evaluating job offers.
- 57% think their company should be doing more to increase diversity among its workforce.

The infographic highlights the importance of diversity in AI innovation by presenting key statistics that show the positive correlation between diverse teams and increased innovation. It provides concrete examples of how diverse inputs improve AI applications in various fields and visually emphasizes the power of inclusivity in driving technological advancements. This visual tool is a powerful affirmation of the benefits of diverse teams in AI development.

By cultivating AI development teams rich in diversity, you are championing a more inclusive tech community and engineering AI solutions that are innovative, equitable, and reflective of the world's rich tapestry. As we continue to explore the multifaceted role of ethics in AI, let this understanding of diversity's value guide your efforts in building teams as varied as the problems you aspire to solve with artificial intelligence.

15.2 Fostering an Ethical Culture in AI Teams

Creating a work environment that inherently promotes ethical behavior and decision-making among AI development teams is akin to cultivating a garden where the healthiest plants thrive. It's about nurturing a space where ethical considerations are as natural as breathing, deeply ingrained in the day-to-day activities of every team member. To achieve this, you must consider the environment a dynamic ecosystem where ethical practices are supported and encouraged through structure, culture, and continuous learning.

Creating an Ethical Work Environment: The foundation of an ethical work environment in AI development begins with clear, actionable policies defining ethical behavior in practice. These policies should cover data handling, privacy considerations, transparency, and mitigating biases in AI algorithms. However, policies alone aren't enough. The physical and psychological aspects of the workplace also play crucial roles. This includes designing workspaces encouraging collaboration and communication and ensuring team members feel safe and valued. Psychological safety, a state where individuals think they can speak up and express their concerns without fear of punishment or humiliation, is particularly crucial. You can foster this by regularly engaging with your team members, seeking their input, and showing genuine interest in their concerns and suggestions.

Additionally, implementing ethical guidelines should be a living process integrated into the fabric of daily work life. This could mean regular ethical checkpoints in project timelines or mandatory ethical reviews before moving on to the next development phase. By making these practices routine, you embed a robust ethical dimension into the workflow, making ethics a continuous presence rather than an afterthought.

Role of Leadership: In fostering an ethical culture, leadership cannot be overstated. Leaders must set ethical standards and live by them, acting as role models for their teams. This involves more than just adhering to ethical practices; it requires leaders to demonstrate commitment through their decisions and behaviors. For instance, when faced with a decision where the ethical choice may delay a project but ensure greater fairness or privacy, leaders must choose the ethical path and explain their reasoning to the team. This transparency in decision-making helps to reinforce the importance of ethics and shows team members that ethical considerations are taken seriously at all levels of the organization.

Leaders should also be accessible to discuss ethical dilemmas and provide guidance. This might involve regular office hours dedicated to discussing ethical concerns or informal coffee chats where team members can speak freely about any issues they're facing. Such practices help build trust and ensure that ethical considerations are woven into the decision-making process at every level.

Training and Awareness: Regular training and awareness programs are essential for maintaining an ethical culture. These programs should cover the organization's policies and the legal aspects of AI ethics and engage with real-world scenarios that team members might face. Interactive workshops where team members can role-play different scenarios or use case studies to explore potential ethical dilemmas can be particularly effective. These sessions should be designed to challenge the participants, encouraging them to think critically and empathetically to navigate complex situations.

Moreover, training programs should be updated regularly to reflect new ethical challenges as AI evolves. This ongoing education ensures that the team's knowledge remains current and they are prepared to handle new situations. It also signals to the team that the organization is committed to ethics and considers it an integral part of professional development.

Encouraging Ethical Dialogue: Promoting an open ethical dialogue within AI teams is crucial. This can be facilitated through regular team meetings to discuss ethical issues encountered in projects. Creating an 'ethical log' where team members can anonymously post questions or concerns about ethical issues they've experienced is another effective strategy. These entries can then be discussed in dedicated sessions, allowing the team to collectively explore solutions and learn from each encounter.

Moreover, establishing a committee or appointing an ethics officer as a point of contact for ethical issues can provide a formal mechanism for raising concerns. This role involves addressing immediate concerns and helping integrate the insights gained from these discussions into the organization's practices and policies.

By embedding these strategies into the core operations of your AI development teams, you create an environment where ethics is not just a compliance requirement but a key driver of innovation and trust. This approach enhances the quality and fairness of the AI solutions developed and positions your organization as a leader in ethical AI development, attracting top talent and building a reputable brand in the tech community.

15.3 Training and Resources for Ethical AI Development

The landscape of artificial intelligence is ever-evolving, and staying updated with the latest ethical practices is beneficial and necessary for any AI professional. A robust educational foundation coupled with continuous learning ensures that AI developers are skilled in technology and champions of ethical standards. This commitment to ongoing education forms the backbone of responsible AI development.

Educational Programs: Numerous universities and educational institutions now offer specialized courses focused on the intersection of AI and ethics. These programs are designed to provide both foundational knowledge and advanced insights into the ethical implications of AI technologies. For instance, courses cover privacy concerns, bias mitigation, sustainable AI practices, and practical sessions on implementing these principles in real-world scenarios. Additionally, these educational programs often include modules on the social impact of AI, preparing developers to think critically about the broader consequences of their work. For professionals already in the field, many institutions offer executive education or short courses tailored to industry veterans looking to update their knowledge or pivot their focus toward ethical AI.

On-the-Job Training: While formal education is invaluable, the dynamic nature of AI development demands practical, on-the-job training. This type of training allows developers to apply ethical concepts directly to their current projects, integrating theory with practice. Companies might conduct regular training sessions where developers can work through ethical dilemmas encountered in their projects, using structured frameworks to explore potential solutions. This approach solidifies understanding and fosters a proactive attitude toward ethical challenges. Moreover, on-the-job training is often more contextual and directly aligned with the company's specific needs, making it an effective tool for addressing unique ethical concerns in different projects.

Online Resources and Communities: The internet is a treasure trove of resources for AI developers seeking to deepen their understanding of AI ethics. Numerous online platforms, forums, and communities offer a space for professionals to learn, discuss, and seek advice on ethical AI development. Websites like AI Ethics Labs provide articles, podcasts, and webinars that delve into current ethical issues in AI. Forums like Stack Exchange have dedicated spaces where developers can pose questions and receive answers from peers and experts worldwide. These online communities serve as educational resources and foster a sense of global camaraderie among AI professionals, encouraging sharing of insights and strategies across borders.

Developing Custom Training Materials: Given AI teams' specific needs and ethical challenges, developing custom training materials can be particularly effective. Tailored training programs allow organizations to address the precise ethical issues relevant to their projects and corporate culture. These materials might include case studies drawn from the company's own experiences, customized ethical dilemmas that reflect the most pressing concerns for the team, and best practices developed from past projects. For instance, a company working on facial recognition technologies might develop training modules that focus extensively on bias identification and mitigation. Customizing materials makes the training more relevant and engaging for the team, leading to better retention and application of ethical practices.

As we conclude this exploration into the essential training and resources for ethical AI development, it's clear that a multifaceted approach is crucial. By combining formal education, practical on-the-job training, utilizing online resources, and developing tailored materials, AI professionals can fully equip themselves to navigate the complex ethical landscape of AI. This comprehensive preparation enhances the integrity and efficacy of AI projects and ensures that the AI community continues to thrive and innovate responsibly. Looking ahead, the next chapter will build upon these foundations, exploring advanced strategies for implementing these ethical practices effectively across various AI applications.

Chapter 16: Strategies for Global

Ethical AI Implementation

Imagine standing at the crossroads of diverse cultures, where the bustling energy of global interaction meets the disciplined silence of boardrooms discussing the future of technology. In the complex dance of international partnerships lies the potential to wield artificial intelligence as a tool for universal ethical advancement. For you, as a developer and thinker in the realm of AI, the act of reaching across geographical and ideological divides to create a unified ethical framework is not just beneficial—it is imperative. This chapter delves into the intricate world of forming global partnerships, a venture crucial not just for ethical uniformity but for pioneering AI systems that are as universally beneficial as they are innovative.

16.1 Establishing Global Partnerships for Ethical AI

Building a Global Ethical AI Framework

The journey toward establishing a global ethical AI framework begins with acknowledging diverse cultural, legal, and social norms that shape AI perceptions and regulations worldwide. The importance of this framework transcends mere regulatory compliance; it is about crafting a mosaic of global ethics that respects and integrates an array of philosophical, cultural, and practical perspectives. Such a framework is not about imposing a one-size-fits-all solution but rather about finding harmony in diversity, ensuring that AI technologies developed in Silicon Valley can be ethically relevant in the streets of Nairobi or the offices of Shanghai.

To achieve this, global partnerships become indispensable. These alliances allow for sharing insights and best practices, ensuring that the ethical standards adopted are inclusive and representative of global needs. Thus, The framework must be robust enough to accommodate legal systems from the stringent GDPR in Europe to the evolving cyber laws in Asia and Africa. It should address core issues such as data privacy, algorithmic transparency, and fairness while being adaptable to accommodate local ethical concerns that may not be universally prominent.

Collaboration Models

Several models of international collaboration can be instrumental in this regard. Multilateral agreements, for instance, bring together multiple countries to negotiate and set common standards, much like the Paris Agreement does for environmental issues. These agreements can outline basic ethical guidelines that all signatory countries agree to implement and enforce within their jurisdictions.

Another effective model is the formation of global consortia comprising AI developers, ethicists, policymakers, and community representatives worldwide. These consortia can function as think tanks, providing ongoing research and recommendations on AI ethics. They can also serve as oversight bodies that monitor the adherence to agreed-upon ethical norms and mediate in cases of disputes or breaches.

International research and development projects also offer a platform for collaborative innovation. Diverse teams work together on AI projects, tackling common global challenges such as healthcare, education, and public safety. These projects lead to technological advancements and foster a deeper understanding and appreciation of diverse ethical viewpoints, promoting a more cohesive approach to AI development.

Overcoming Challenges

However, the path to successful global partnerships in AI ethics is fraught with challenges. Geopolitical tensions can influence or hinder collaboration efforts, with countries viewing AI advancements through the lens of national security and competitive advantage. Differing regulatory landscapes and economic disparities between developed and developing nations also pose significant hurdles. Due to resource constraints, developing countries might need help implementing advanced AI technologies and ethical frameworks, requiring more substantial support and investment from their developed counterparts.

A commitment to openness, mutual respect, and shared goals is crucial to navigating these challenges. Initiatives like technology transfer, shared research funding, and capacity-building programs can help level the playing field, allowing for more equitable participation in global AI ethics development.

Success Stories

Despite these challenges, there are success stories that illuminate the potential of global partnerships. For example, the Global AI Safety Alliance (GASA) stands out as a beacon of successful collaboration. Comprising AI researchers from over 30 countries, GASA has developed a dynamic ethical AI framework that numerous international tech firms have adopted. Their approach to continuous dialogue and consensus-building has enabled them to update their ethical guidelines bi-annually, reflecting new developments and challenges in AI technology.

Another notable success is the AI for Good initiative, launched by a consortium of tech giants. This initiative has implemented AI-based solutions to address urgent global issues like hunger and disease outbreak predictions. By pooling resources, expertise, and data from across continents, this initiative has advanced ethical AI development and demonstrated the tangible benefits of AI in solving humanitarian challenges.

Visual Element: Global AI Ethics Framework Infographic

An infographic that outlines the structure of a typical global AI ethics framework, illustrating critical components like data rights, transparency measures, and fairness protocols. It also highlights the roles of various stakeholders, including governments, tech companies, and civil society, in shaping and maintaining this framework.

Figure 10 - Global Ethical Framework

Icon Descriptions:

1. **Data Rights**:

   - **Icon**: A lock symbol over a data file.

   - **Description**: Represents the protection and management of data rights, ensuring privacy and security.

2. **Transparency Measures**:

- **Icon**: An eye over a document.
- **Description**: Denotes the importance of transparency in AI operations and decision-making processes.

3. **Fairness Protocols**:
   - **Icon**: Scales of justice.
   - **Description**: Symbolizes the need for fairness and equality in AI systems, ensuring unbiased outcomes.

4. **Governments**:
   - **Icon**: A government building.
   - **Description**: Highlights the role of governments in regulating and enforcing AI ethics standards.

5. **Tech Companies**:
   - **Icon**: A computer or tech building.
   - **Description**: Represents the responsibility of tech companies in developing and maintaining ethical AI technologies.

6. **Civil Society**:
   - **Icon**: People holding hands.
   - **Description**: Emphasizes the involvement of civil society in advocating for ethical AI

practices and holding stakeholders accountable.

Summary:

This infographic provides a clear and organized visual representation of a global AI ethics framework. It outlines critical components such as data rights, transparency measures, and fairness protocols while highlighting various stakeholders, including governments, tech companies, and civil society, who shape and maintain this framework.

Navigating the complexities of global ethical AI implementation puts you at the forefront of a movement seeking to advance technology and ensure it serves humanity equitably and conscientiously. As this chapter unfolds, it becomes evident that the collective effort in bridging diverse ethical landscapes through robust partnerships is not merely an academic exercise but a practical necessity, shaping the future of AI in a globally interconnected world.

16.2 Case Study:
Successful Global AI Ethics Implementation

In the evolving landscape of global AI ethics, the AI-Language Equity Initiative (ALEI) is a standout project that exemplifies successful implementation. This project, spearheaded by a consortium of technology firms, academic institutions, and nonprofit organizations spanning four continents, aimed to develop and deploy AI systems that could provide real-time language translation and literacy tools across underserved languages globally. The partners involved ranged from tech giants in Silicon Valley and Bangalore to universities in Cairo and non-profile non-government organizations (NGOs) in Brazil, each bringing a unique perspective and expertise. This diversity was crucial, as the project's core mission was to bridge communication gaps that often exacerbate social and economic disparities.

Ethical Frameworks Applied

The ethical backbone of ALEI was grounded in principles of inclusivity, fairness, and respect for cultural diversity. From the outset, the consortium established a multilayered ethical framework that guided every project phase. This framework was not merely about compliance with global data protection laws but was deeply rooted in a commitment to respecting and preserving linguistic diversity. One of the critical aspects of this framework was the integration of local ethical norms and values into the AI development process. For instance, the AI models were trained not just to translate languages but to understand and convey cultural nuances, which is critical in maintaining the integrity and richness of indigenous languages.

This respect for cultural differences was also evident in the consortium's approach to data collection. Community-based participatory research methods were employed, involving local stakeholders in the data-gathering process to ensure that the data used to train AI models were rich and diverse and collected in a manner that respects community norms and privacy expectations. This approach helped mitigate potential biases in AI algorithms, which could otherwise have led to oversimplified or inaccurate translations, potentially reinforcing stereotypes or misrepresentations.

Outcomes and Impact

The impact of ALEI was multifaceted, reflecting the broad ethical considerations embedded in the project. The initiative provided essential education, healthcare, and commerce tools for communities that previously needed more access to digital resources due to language barriersThis was particularly evident in the regular ethical review sessions conducted by the consortium, where partners would discuss challenges and learn from each other's experiences and perspectives. For example, in rural areas of East Africa, the AI-powered apps developed through ALEI enabled local farmers to access real-time market information and agricultural tips in Swahili and several other regional languages, significantly boosting their productivity and market reach.

The ethical impact on the AI community was equally profound. The project served as a powerful case study of how AI can be developed and deployed in a manner that genuinely respects and enhances human dignity and cultural diversity. It demonstrated the viability of ethical AI frameworks beyond token compliance and genuinely integrating local values and norms into technology development.

Additionally, the collaborative nature of the project fostered a greater understanding and appreciation of ethical diversity among the global partners. This was particularly evident in the regular ethical review sessions conducted by the consortium, where partners discussed challenges and learned from each other's experiences and perspectives. These sessions were instrumental in continuously refining the ethical frameworks applied in the project, ensuring they remained dynamic and responsive to new insights and challenges.

Scalability and Replicability

The scalability and replicability of ALEI's approach are among its most compelling attributes. The project demonstrated that with a robust ethical foundation and a commitment to genuine collaboration, AI initiatives can be scaled to address global challenges while respecting local norms and values. The frameworks and methodologies developed through ALEI have been documented in a series of white papers and toolkits, and they are now publicly available for other organizations to adapt and apply in their AI projects.

ALEI is a blueprint for future global AI initiatives and how ethical considerations can be seamlessly integrated into technology development. It underscores the importance of involving diverse stakeholders in the design and implementation phases and maintaining an agile ethical review process that can evolve with the project. Moreover, ALEI's success illustrates the potential for ethical AI to not only prevent harm but actively contribute to social good, bridging gaps that have long hindered equitable development across the globe.

16.3 The Role of AI in Bridging Global Inequalities

In a world where wealth, health, and education disparities cast long shadows across continents, AI emerges as a beacon of hope, potentially leveling the playing field for millions. As you, the AI developer, engineer, or ethicist, engage with this transformative technology, it's crucial to steer its application towards reducing these global inequalities rather than inadvertently widening them. AI can analyze vast amounts of data for insights that can improve lives, making it a powerful tool for equity if directed conscientiously.

AI's role in addressing economic disparities is profound. Consider financial services, where AI can enhance access to credit in underserved markets. Traditionally, individuals in low-income regions need a more formal financial history, which bars them from traditional banking services. AI-driven models can predict creditworthiness based on alternative data, such as mobile phone usage patterns and utility payments, thus broadening access to finance. This is more than an operational tweak. It's a gateway to economic empowerment for millions, allowing them to start businesses, improve their homes, and invest in their futures.

However, deploying AI in such critical sectors necessitates stringent ethical considerations to ensure fairness and prevent exploitation. AI systems must be meticulously designed to avoid reinforcing or creating new biases. This involves diverse training data accurately reflecting the global population and continuous monitoring to swiftly identify and rectify bias or unfair outcomes. Transparency in how AI makes decisions, especially in high-stakes areas like credit scoring, is crucial for maintaining trust and accountability.

The impact of AI in bridging healthcare disparities is similarly transformative but requires careful ethical management. Remote areas with sparse healthcare facilities can benefit immensely from AI-powered diagnostic tools and telemedicine services. These technologies can bring expert-level diagnostics to corners of the world where even essential medical advice was previously hard to come by. For instance, AI algorithms that analyze images to detect diseases such as tuberculosis or diabetic retinopathy are already changing lives in Africa and Asia. Yet, the ethical deployment of such AI applications must ensure that they complement rather than replace human healthcare providers, integrate local healthcare practices and preferences, and maintain patient privacy and data security at all times.

Education is another frontier where AI can significantly reduce global inequalities. AI educational platforms can provide personalized learning experiences to students in under-resourced areas, adapting to each student's learning pace and style. This can help bridge the educational divide by offering high-quality, accessible education to students regardless of their geographical location. However, to ensure these AI systems do not perpetuate educational inequalities, they must be free from cultural biases and accessible to students without requiring high-end infrastructure.

Guidelines for Equitable AI Development

Developing AI with an equity lens involves several vital guidelines that ensure the technology benefits all sections of global society. Firstly, diverse stakeholders should be involved in designing and deploying AI systems. This includes technologists, local community leaders, social workers, and end-users. Their insights can ensure that AI solutions are culturally sensitive and practically applicable to the problems they aim to solve.

Secondly, transparency and understandability in AI systems should be prioritized. Users should be able to understand how AI decisions are made, especially when these decisions impact their economic, health, or educational status. This transparency builds trust and allows users to challenge and seek redress against potentially harmful AI-driven decisions.

Thirdly, commit to ongoing monitoring and evaluation of AI impacts. This is crucial to ensure that AI systems operate fairly and effectively as they scale across different regions and populations. Regular impact assessments help identify unintended consequences of AI deployment, allowing for timely adjustments.

Lastly, global cooperation should be fostered in developing ethical AI standards. No single organization or country has all the answers. Collaborative efforts can lead to the creation of robust, universally applicable ethical guidelines that consider the varied facets of human experience.

When harnessed with meticulous attention to ethical considerations, AI holds the promise of a more equitable world. As this chapter integrates into the broader narrative of the book, it ties the potent capabilities of AI with the moral imperatives of equity and justice, urging you to partake in this technological evolution thoughtfully and responsibly. By embedding principles of fairness and inclusivity into the core of AI development, you contribute to advancing technology and crafting a future where technology serves humanity's broadest aspirations.

Make a Difference with Your Review

Thanks to your feedback, support, and reviews, I'm able to create the best books possible and serve more people.

I would be extremely grateful if you could take just 60 seconds to kindly leave an honest review of the book on Amazon. Please share your feedback and thoughts for others to see.

To do so, scan the QR code to share your thoughts. Select a star rating and write a couple of sentences. That's it!

I hope I have helped you understand the importance of Ethical Artificial Intelligence and will use what you have learned to help improve the AI used all over the world.

Thank you from the bottom of my heart.

Debbie Sue Jancis

Conclusion

As we draw this exploration to a close, let us reflect on the profound journey we have embarked upon, traversing the intricate landscape of artificial intelligence ethics. From the foundational theories and historical milestones that shape our understanding of AI ethics to the robust ethical frameworks and practical applications discussed, this book has aimed to illuminate the critical role of ethics in the realm of AI.

Throughout these pages, we have delved into the essential considerations that must guide AI innovation to prevent a dystopian future where unintended consequences mar technology's potential. We've uncovered the indispensable value of ethical frameworks as tools for responsible AI development, discussed proactive strategies for addressing common ethical pitfalls like bias and data privacy, and emphasized the importance of cultural sensitivity in our increasingly interconnected global initiatives.

The message is clear: Ethical AI is not merely a philosophical ideal but a practical necessity for sustainable progress. As technology races ahead, the stakes of overlooking this crucial aspect rise, threatening to overshadow AI's benefits with potential harms. This book has been crafted to inform and equip you—developers, project managers, ethicists, and all stakeholders in the AI field—with the tools, frameworks, and mindsets necessary to implement ethical AI in your projects and organizations.

Please to take personal and professional responsibility for weaving ethical considerations into the fabric of your AI endeavors. Engage actively with the broader ethical AI community through forums, workshops, and professional networks. Stay informed and contribute to ongoing discussions that shape this evolving field. Remember, the landscape of AI ethics is continually transforming, with new challenges and solutions emerging as technology advances. We must remain vigilant, ensuring our ethical frameworks keep pace with technological innovation.

Looking ahead, I am optimistic about AI's potential to enhance human capabilities, enrich our lives, and address some of the most pressing global challenges—provided we commit to developing and using this technology ethically. View yourselves as pioneers on the ethical frontier of AI, shaping a future where technology aligns with humanity's highest values and aspirations.

Finally, I invite you to join this ongoing conversation. Share your experiences, challenges, and successes in implementing ethical AI practices. Your insights and feedback are invaluable as we strive to foster a community of ethical AI practitioners.

Together, let us champion the cause of ethical AI and secure a future that honors our deepest commitments to fairness, integrity, and respect for all. Thank you for joining me on this essential journey.

Common Slang / Lingo:

1. **AI (Artificial Intelligence)**: Refers to computer systems or machines that mimic human intelligence to perform tasks and can iteratively improve themselves based on the information they collect.

2. **ML (Machine Learning)** is a subset of AI. It's the process of training a computer system to make decisions or predictions based on data without being explicitly programmed for each specific task.

3. **Deep Learning**: A subset of ML that involves neural networks with many layers. It's used for more complex tasks like image and speech recognition.

4. **Neural Network**: Inspired by the human brain, this is a series of algorithms that attempts to recognize underlying relationships in a data set through a process that mimics human brain operations.

5. **Algorithm**: A set of rules or instructions given to an AI, computer program, or system to help in problem-solving or decision-making.

6. **Big Data**: Enormous data sets that may be analyzed computationally to reveal patterns, trends, and

associations, especially those relating to human behavior and interactions.

7. **NLP (Natural Language Processing)**: A field of AI that allows machines to read, understand, and derive meaning from human languages.

8. **API (Application Programming Interface)**: A set of rules and tools for building software applications that specify how software components should interact.

9. **Data Mining**: The practice of examining large databases to generate new information and find patterns

10. **Cloud Computing**: The delivery of different services through the Internet, including data storage, servers, databases, networking, and software.

11. **Agile Development**: A software development methodology that involves the continuous iteration of development and testing in the software development process.

12. **Blockchain**: A system of recording information that makes it difficult or impossible to change, hack, or cheat the system. It's a digital ledger of transactions duplicated and distributed across the entire network of computer systems on the blockchain.

13. **Quantum Computing**: A type of computing that takes advantage of quantum phenomena like superposition and quantum entanglement. This emerging technology could perform specific computational tasks much faster than classical computers.

References

Borenstein, J., Grodzinsky, F. S., Howard, A., Miller, K. W., & Wolf, M. J. (2021). AI ethics: a long history and a recent burst of attention. *Computer*, *54*(1), 96–102. https://doi.org/10.1109/mc.2020.3034950

Saheb, T. (2024). Mapping Ethical Artificial Intelligence Policy Landscape: A Mixed Method analysis. *Science and Engineering Ethics*, *30*(2). https://doi.org/10.1007/s11948-024-00472-6

Ethics of Artificial Intelligence and Robotics (Stanford Encyclopedia of Philosophy). (2020, April 30). https://plato.stanford.edu/entries/ethics-ai/

Engler, A., Renda, A., Kerry, C. F., Meltzer, J. P., & Fanni, R. (2021, October 25). Strengthening international cooperation on AI. *Brookings*. https://www.brookings.edu/articles/strengthening-international-cooperation-on-ai/

Luiza Jarovsky. (2023, March 19). *Privacy by Design in the Age of AI, with Dr. Ann Cavoukian* [Video]. YouTube. https://www.youtube.com/watch?v=gW-erhQIFik

Mitigating bias in artificial Intelligence - Berkeley Haas. (2024, May 13). Berkeley Haas. https://haas.berkeley.edu/equity/resources/playbooks/mitigating-bias-in-ai/

World Health Organization: WHO. (2023, May 16). WHO calls for safe and ethical AI for health. *World Health Organization*.

https://www.who.int/news/item/16-05-2023-who-calls-for-safe-and-ethical-ai-for-health

United Nations Environment Programme. (n.d.). *How artificial intelligence is helping tackle environmental challenges.* UNEP. https://www.unep.org/news-and-stories/story/how-artificial-intelligence-helping-tackle-environmental-challenges

Global AI regulation: A closer look at the US, EU, and China. (n.d.). Transcend. https://transcend.io/blog/ai-regulation

Case studies. (2019, April 24). Princeton Dialogues on AI and Ethics. https://aiethics.princeton.edu/case-studies/

Defense Advanced Research Projects Agency - Content not found. (n.d.). https://www.darpa.mil/program/explainable-artificial-intelligence/

Kiiski, K. (2023, December 15). *Cultural Relativism in AI Ethics: Navigating the complex terrain.* https://www.linkedin.com/pulse/cultural-relativism-ai-ethics-navigating-complex-terrain-kiiski-zmumf

Admin, & Shashkina, V. (2023, May 11). *What is AI bias really, and how can you combat it?* ITRex. https://itrexgroup.com/blog/ai-bias-definition-types-examples-debiasing-strategies/

Chin, M. H., Afsar-Manesh, N., Bierman, et. Al (2023b). Guiding principles to address the impact of algorithm bias on racial and ethnic disparities in health and health care. *JAMA Network Open*, *6*(12), e2345050. https://doi.org/10.1001/jamanetworkopen.2023.450 50

Google AI. (n.d.-b). *Google Responsible AI Practices – Google AI.* https://ai.google/responsibility/responsible-ai-practices/

Polli, F. (2023, January 18). *Using AI to Eliminate Bias from Hiring.* Harvard Business Review. https://hbr.org/2019/10/using-ai-to-eliminate-bias-from-hiring

Global AI Law and Policy Tracker. (n.d.). https://iapp.org/resources/article/global-ai-legislation-tracker/

Yu, L., & Li, Y. (2022). Artificial intelligence Decision-Making transparency and employees' trust: The parallel multiple mediating effect of effectiveness and discomfort. *Behavioral Sciences*, *12*(5), 127. https://doi.org/10.3390/bs12050127

Filipsson, F., & Filipsson, F. (2024, March 11). Predicting the Future AI: Trends in Artificial intelligence. *Redress Compliance - Just another WordPress site.* https://redresscompliance.com/predicting-the-future-ai-trends-in-artificial-intelligence/#:~:text=What%20future%20trends%20should%20we,responsible%20evolution%20of%20AI%20technologies

AI will transform the global economy. let's make sure it benefits humanity. (2024, January 14). IMF. https://www.imf.org/en/Blogs/Articles/2024/01/14/ai-will-transform-the-global-economy-lets-make-sure-it-benefits-humanity

Kuziemski, M., & Misuraca, G. (2020). AI governance in the public sector: Three tales from the frontiers of automated decision-making in democratic settings. *Telecommunications Policy*, *44*(6), 101976. https://doi.org/10.1016/j.telpol.2020.101976

De La Torre James Frazee, A. (2024, April 4). *A call to action to address inequity in AI access (opinion).* Inside Higher Ed | Higher Education News, Events and Jobs. https://www.insidehighered.com/opinion/views/2024/04/04/call-action-address-inequity-ai-access-opinion

Alagar. (2024b, May 14). AI for Good: Tackling Global Challenges with Artificial Intelligence. *IABAC®.* https://iabac.org/blog/ai-for-good-tackling-global-challenges-with-artificial-intelligence

Unesco. (n.d.). *Ethics of Artificial Intelligence.* Unesco.org. Retrieved July 3, 2024, from https://www.unesco.org/en/artificial-intelligence/recommendation-ethics/

James, S. (2023, September 20). *Age of AI: Why organizations need a Chief Ethics Officer.* https://www.informationweek.com/machine-learning-ai/age-of-ai-why-organizations-need-a-chief-ethics-officer#close-modal

How businesses can create ethical culture in the age of tech. (2021, March 5). World Economic Forum. https://www.weforum.org/agenda/2020/01/how-businesses-can-create-an-ethical-culture-in-the-age-of-tech/

Weitzman, T. (2023, December 14). The Ethics of AI: Balancing innovation and responsibility. *Forbes.* https://www.forbes.com/sites/forbesbusinesscouncil/2023/12/14/the-ethics-of-ai-balancing-innovation-and-responsibility/

Innodata. (2021, December 2). *Best Approaches to mitigate bias in AI Models.* Innodata Inc. https://innodata.com/best-approaches-to-mitigate-bias-in-ai-models/

Okolo, C. T. (2023, November 1). AI in the Global South: Opportunities and challenges towards more inclusive governance. *Brookings.* https://www.brookings.edu/articles/ai-in-the-global-south-opportunities-and-challenges-towards-more-inclusive-governance/#:~:text=Within%20agriculture%2C%20projects%20have%20focused,support%20precision%20agriculture%20and%20forest

Miah, A. (n.d.). *Ethics issues raised by human enhancement | OpenMind.* OpenMind. https://www.bbvaopenmind.com/en/articles/ethics-issues-raised-by-human-enhancement/

Lethal Autonomous Weapon Systems (LAWS) – UNODA. (n.d.). https://disarmament.unoda.org/the-convention-on-certain-conventional-weapons/background-on-laws-in-the-ccw/

NASA Artificial Intelligence Ethics - NASA. (n.d.). NASA. https://www.nasa.gov/nasa-artificial-intelligence-ethics/

Santa Clara University. (n.d.). *Teaching a course on AI ethics as part of Engineering/CS curricula.* Markkula Center for Applied Ethics. https://www.scu.edu/ethics/focus-areas/technology-ethics/resources/embedding-ethics-into-computing-curricula-resources-and-suggestions/teaching-a-course-on-ai-ethics-as-part-of-engineeringcs-curricula/

SITNFlash. (2020, October 26). *Racial discrimination in face recognition technology - Science in the news.* Science in the News. https://sitn.hms.harvard.edu/flash/2020/racial-discrimination-in-face-recognition-technology/

Jessica. (2022, May 13). *The AI Ethics Boom: 150 Ethical AI Startups and Industry Trends - BGV.* BGV. https://benhamouglobalventures.com/ai-ethics-boom-150-ethical-ai-startups-industry-trends/

Peter Leshaw Digital Marketing: Strategies and Training. (2023, April 19). *NLP (Natural Language Processing) Definitions - Peter Leshaw Digital Marketing: Strategies and training.* https://peterleshaw.com/nlp-natural-language-processing-definitions/

Stark, L. (2023). Breaking Up (with) AI Ethics. *American Literature*, *95*(2), 365–379. https://doi.org/10.1215/00029831-10575148

Risk Management Studio. (2019, November 18). *Information Security–vs–Cybersecurity*. https://www.riskmanagementstudio.com/information-security-vs-cybersecurity/

Sus, V. (2023, September 6). Normative Ethics Theories (with Examples) (2024). *Helpful Professor*. https://helpfulprofessor.com/normative-ethics-theories/

Roe, D. (2018, November 14). Stop Thinking AI vs. Human, Think AI With Human. *CMSWire.com*. https://www.cmswire.com/digital-workplace/stop-thinking-ai-vs-human-think-ai-with-human/

Decoding the rise of Self-Driving Vehicles - www.sportsmanpilot.com. (2023, August 5). http://www.sportsmanpilot.com/decoding-the-rise-of-self-driving-vehicles

Duignan, B. (2024, May 31). *Trolley problem | Definition, Variations, Arguments, Solutions, & Facts*. Encyclopedia Britannica. https://www.britannica.com/topic/trolley-problem

Guide to GDPR Privacy By Design and Default: Checklist. (n.d.). https://www.strac.io/blog/guide-to-gdpr-privacy-by-design-and-default-checklist

Mort, J. (2024, January 17). *How 'Gender Shades' sheds light on bias in machine learning*. DPAS.

https://www.dataprivacyadvisory.com/how-gender-shades-sheds-light-on-bias-in-machine-learning/

AI Fairness 360. (n.d.). IBM Developer. https://www.ibm.com/opensource/open/projects/ai-fairness-360/

An Introduction to AI: A Glimpse into the Future of Technology | Kenility. (2024, August 26). Kenility. https://www.kenility.com/blog/technology/introduction-ai-glimpse-future-technology

Self-Driving Cars: the intersection of tech and ethics. (2023, October 21). http://www.companion-software.com/self-driving-cars-the-intersection-of-tech-and-ethics

Infographic: How Diversity drives Business Success. (n.d.-b). SCORE. https://www.score.org/resource/infographic/infographic-how-diversity-drives-business-success

Needed, C. (2019b, July 24). *The Trolley Problem.* Citation Needed. https://www.citationpod.com/the-trolley-problem/

Siteadmin. (2022, August 5). *Follow the steps in the Markkula Center for Applied Ethics Making an Ethical Decision framework.* Homework Crew. https://homeworkcrew.com/2022/08/05/follow-the-steps-in-the-markkula-center-for-applied-ethics-making-an-ethical-decision-framework

Hosken, M. (2023, September 5). *Privacy by Design and its 7 principles You must know about.* WebsitePolicies. https://www.websitepolicies.com/blog/privacy-by-design

themesflat.com. (n.d.). *Informed consent in Data Protection.* https://www.bcaa.uk/informed-consent-in-data-protection.html

The impact of the internet on our world: From communication to commerce. (n.d.). The Swamp. https://vocal.media/theSwamp/the-impact-of-the-internet-on-our-world-from-communication-to-commerce

Web, F. T. (2023, April 17). 27 jobs at risk of being replaced by AI. *ResumeOK.* https://www.resumeok.com/27-jobs-being-replaced-ai/

Roller, J. (2023, July 17). *The 10 latest artificial intelligence trends that your business needs to embrace.* IEEE Computer Society. https://www.computer.org/publications/tech-news/trends/the-latest-artificial-intelligence-trends-to-embrace/

About the Author

Debbie Sue Jancis is a dynamic, seasoned leader and a passionate advocate for both AI development and ethical leadership. With over three decades of experience in Engineering Management at high-tech companies like Oracle, eBay, Symantec, Intuit, and IBM, Debbie has honed a deep technical expertise, particularly in artificial intelligence (AI) and its ethical applications in modern society. Her passion for AI stems from a desire to advance technology while ensuring that ethical considerations remain at the forefront of its development and implementation.

In addition to her technical prowess, Debbie holds a Bachelor of Science in Computer Science from Syracuse University. She has used her expertise to demystify complex concepts in AI, making them accessible to professionals across industries. Her books are known for blending technical depth with practical insights, providing readers with the tools to navigate leadership and ethical dilemmas in the rapidly evolving world of AI.

Debbie is also deeply committed to empowering individuals in their leadership journeys. She has authored several books that provide actionable advice for those aspiring to or currently in leadership positions, with a strong focus on ethical behavior in technology-driven environments. Her mission is to unlock the potential within each individual, believing that ethical leadership and AI development can coexist to create a better future.

Moreover, with over 25 years of volunteering for the Boy Scouts of America, Debbie has applied the leadership knowledge and ethical principles the BSA taught in her everyday life and her professional career. She is dedicated to spreading the belief that strong, ethical leadership—especially in AI—is the cornerstone of successful organizations.

Known for her engaging and motivational style, Debbie's works have become essential reading for professionals eager to enhance their leadership skills, drive change in AI development, and inspire their teams to achieve greatness while navigating the ethical challenges of the modern technological landscape.

Also available from JFE Publishing:

Debbie Sue Jancis:

Leadership / Management:

- Management in the New World: Pocket Guide To Managing Remote Teams
- Virtuous Leadership Skills: Easily Lead with Integrity and Emotional Intelligence for Effective Decision Making, Time

Puzzle / Coloring Books:

- The Ultimate Sudoku Collection: Puzzles to Sooth and Sharpen Your Mind
- Cats and Kittens: 55 cute Cats and Kittens Coloring Book for Relaxation and Stress Relief
- Splendors of Spring Activity Book for Adults: Including Crosswords, Sudoku, Word Search, Mazes, and More

Alex & Susan James:

Science Fiction:

- Code Countdown – Grace Kim Mystery, Book 1
- Code Legacy – Grace Kim Mystery, Book 2

Made in United States
Troutdale, OR
11/15/2024

24882837R00169